Web Style Guide

Web Style Guide

Basic Design Principles for Creating Web Sites

Patrick J. Lynch
Yale University Center for Advanced Instructional Media

Sarah Horton
Dartmouth College

Yale University Press
New Haven and London

Library of Congress Cataloging-in-Publication Data

Lynch, Patrick J., 1953–
    Web style guide : basic design principles for creating web sites / by
Patrick J. Lynch, Sarah Horton.
        p.   cm.
    Includes bibliographical references (p.   ) and index.
    ISBN 0-300-07674-6 (cloth : alk. paper). – ISBN 0-300-07675-4
(paper : alk. paper)
    1. Web sites – Design. 1. Horton, Sarah, 1962– . 11. Title.
TK5105.888.L96   1999
005.7'2 – dc21   98-45282
                                                                CIP

A catalogue record for this book is available from the British Library.

The paper in this book meets the guidelines for permanence and durability
of the Committee on Production Guidelines for Book Longevity
of the Council on Library Resources.

10 9 8 7 6

For Cheryl and Devorah
-PL

For my son (sun), Nico
-SH

Contents

Preface

THIS BOOK IS FOR ALL THOSE who wish to publish durable content on the Web. Durable content is not guided by trends; good design will withstand the test of time, whereas trends quickly become frivolous. Success in Web design goes beyond technology and fashion. To create Web sites that endure you need only to communicate your ideas clearly and effectively to your readers.

Though still young, the World Wide Web has already undergone several transformations. The framers of the Web were scientists who wanted to create a device-independent method for exchanging documents. They devised HTML (HyperText Markup Language) as a method for "marking up" the structure of documents to allow for exchange and comparison. Their focus was on the structural logic of documents, not the visual logic of graphic design.

But the Web quickly caught on as a publishing medium; no communication device is more inexpensive or far-reaching. As a tool for communication, however, Web authoring with HTML has limitations. With their focus on the structure of documents, the originators of the Web ignored those visual aspects of information delivery that are critical to effective communication. Once the Web was established as a viable publishing medium, these limitations became obvious and cumbersome. Pages that conformed to HTML standards lacked visual appeal, showing little evidence of the past five centuries of progress in print design. Graphic designers took this relatively primitive authoring and layout tool and began to bend and adapt it to a purpose it was never intended to serve: graphic page design.

The Web viewing audience was also beginning to refine its tastes. The pioneering Web "surfers" who were content to skim the surface of Internet documents are now outnumbered. People are turning to the Web for information – information with depth, breadth, and integrity.

Our purpose for writing this book is to offer basic design principles that you can use to make your content as easy to understand as possible. We explain how to use design as a tool, not as an objective; your Web design should be almost transparent to the reader. We show you how to create a user interface that will allow visitors to your site to navigate your content with ease. We offer suggestions on how to write Web documents; this is a new genre with its own style and guidelines. We delve deep into Web images – color, resolution, compression, and formats – and discuss the benefits of publishing images on the Web. We cover the stylistic and technical issues surrounding the addition of dynamic media to your Web site. All the guidance we offer shares a single purpose: to make your message clear to your readers.

This is not an HTML manual, nor is it a book on graphic design. It is a practical guide to help you design Web sites for the long run.

Many people have given generously of their time and advice during the preparation of this book and of the Web site that preceded the book. At Yale University Press we extend our warmest thanks to Jean Thomson Black, Laura Jones Dooley, and James J. Johnson. We also thank Craig Locatis, Donald Norman, and Edward Tufte for their valuable contributions.

I extend heartfelt thanks to my friends and colleagues at Yale University Center for Advanced Instructional Media: Carl Jaffe, Phillip Simon, Sean Jackson, Kimberly Pasko, Marsha Vazquez, and Jeff Colket. In particular, I'd like to thank Carl Jaffe for over ten years of friendship, wise counsel, and practical advice, much of which now appears on these pages. I'd also like to acknowledge and thank my co-author and good friend Sarah Horton for her friendship, for her partnership in this enterprise, and for convincing me that converting our *Web Style Guide* site into a book was a good idea.

I am especially grateful to the following individuals for their comments, suggestions, assistance, and counsel over the development of this book and companion Web site: Anne Altemus, Emmett Barkley, Richard Beebe, David Bolinsky, Stephen Cohen, Frank Gallo, Kathryn Latimer, Howard Newstadt, Noble Proctor, Lynna Stone-Infeld, Jan Taylor, Mi Young Toh, Tom Urtz, and Cheryl Warfield.

-PL

I thank my co-author, Patrick Lynch, for asking me to join him as co-author of the second edition of the online *Web Style Guide*. Little did he know where that invitation would lead, and I am grateful for his unfailing friendship and good humor throughout the development of this book. I am deeply indebted to Pat and his colleagues at Yale University Center for Advanced Instructional Media for taking me in some years back and teaching me how to see.

I am indebted to my many colleagues and friends at Dartmouth College for their support, suggestions, and counsel, especially John Hawkins, Sheila Culbert, D. Randall Spydell, Ned Holbrook, and Robert M. Murray. I also thank the faculty whose sites appear in this book: Joan Campbell, Eva Fodor, Sally Hair, Allen Koop, Thomas Luxon, and Gerard Russo.

I also thank Malcolm Brown for his steadfast support.

-SH

1   *Process*

A garden is finished when there is nothing left to remove.
– Zen aphorism

THE FIRST STEP in designing any Web site is to define your goals. Without a clearly stated mission and objectives the project will drift, bog down, or continue past an appropriate endpoint. Careful planning and a clear purpose are the keys to success in building Web sites, particularly when you are working as part of a development team.

BEFORE YOU BEGIN

Web sites are generally developed by groups of people: content experts, writers, information architects, graphic designers, technical experts, and a producer or committee chair responsible for seeing the project to completion. Here are questions to address as you start to develop a complex Web site:

- What is the mission of your organization?
- How will creating a Web site support your mission?
- What are your immediate goals for the site?
- What are your long-term goals for the site?
- What Web-related strategies will you use to achieve those goals?
- How will you measure the success of your site?

These are big questions, and the broad conceptual issues are too often dismissed as committees push toward starting the "real work" of designing and building a Web site. However, if you cannot confidently answer all of these questions, then no amount of design or production effort can guarantee a useful result.

WHAT ARE YOUR GOALS?

A short statement identifying two or three goals should be the foundation of your Web site design. The statement should include specific strategies around which the Web site will be designed, how long the site design, construction, and evaluation periods will be, and specific quantitative and qualitative measures of how the success of the site will be evaluated. Building a Web site is an ongoing process, not a one-time project with static content. Long-term editorial management and technical maintenance must be covered in your budget and production plans for the site. Without this perspective your electronic publication will suffer the same fate as many corporate communications initiatives – an enthusiastic start without lasting accomplishments.

KNOW YOUR AUDIENCE

The next step is to identify the potential readers of your Web site so that you can structure the site design to meet their needs and expectations. The knowledge, background, interests, and needs of users will vary from tentative novices who need a carefully structured introduction to expert "power users" who may chafe at anything that seems to patronize them or delay their access to information. A well-designed system should be able to accommodate a range of users' skills and interests. For example, if the goal of your Web site is to deliver internal corporate information, human resources documents, or other information formerly published in paper manuals, your audience will range from those who will visit the site many times every day to those who refer only occasionally to the site.

Web surfers Home pages aimed at browsers should be analogous to magazine covers. The objective is to entice the casual browser with a compelling mix of graphics and clear statements about content. All the links on your home page should point inward, toward pages within your site. Provide concise statements of what is in the site that might interest the reader.

Novice and occasional users These users depend on an unambiguous structure and easy access to overviews that illustrate how information is arranged within your Web site. Novices tend to be intimidated by complex text menus and may be tentative about delving into the site if the home page is not attractive and clearly arranged. Infrequent users benefit from overview pages, hierarchical maps, and design graphics and icons that will trigger their memory about where information is stored within the site. A glossary of technical terms, acronyms, abbreviations, and a list of "frequently asked questions" (FAQs) can be helpful to first-time or infrequent users. This group is always a concern for designers, but their numbers are shrinking daily as the Web becomes a mainstream business tool.

Expert and frequent users These users depend on your site to obtain information quickly and accurately. Expert users are generally impatient with multiple low-density graphic menus that offer only a few choices at a time. Power users crave stripped-down, fast-loading text menus. Graphic froufrou drives them nuts. Expert and frequent users generally have specific goals in mind and will appreciate detailed text menus, site structure outlines, comprehensive site indexes, and well-designed search engines that permit fast search and retrieval. Lots of users now fall in this category. Even if your enterprise is just adopting the Web for internal communication you may be surprised at how much of your audience is thoroughly familiar with the Web.

International users   Remember that you are designing for the *World Wide* Web. Your readers could be the people down the hall or people in Australia or Poland. To reach the maximum number of users in foreign countries you may need to provide translations, at least of your key menu pages. Avoid idiosyncratic professional jargon or obscure technical acronyms in your introductory or explanatory pages. Don't assume that every reader will follow your date and time conventions. For example, don't abbreviate dates on your Web pages. To an American, "3/4/99" reads as "March 4, 1999," but readers in most other countries would read the abbreviated date as "3 April 1999."

DESIGN CRITIQUES

Each member of a site development team will bring different goals, preferences, and skills to the project. Once the team has reached agreement on the mission and goals of the project, consensus on the overall design approach for the Web site needs to be established. The goal at this stage to identify potential successful models in other Web sites and to begin to *see the design problem from the site user's point of view.*

Unfortunately, production teams rarely include members of the target audience for the Web site. And it is often difficult for team members who are not already experienced site designers to articulate their specific preferences, except in reference to existing sites. Group critiques are a great way to explore what makes a Web site successful, because everyone on the team sees each site from a user's point of view. Have each team member bring a list of a few favorite sites to the critique, and ask them to introduce their sites and comment on the successful elements of each design. In this way you will learn one another's design sensibilities and begin to build consensus on the experience your audience will have when they visit the finished site.

CONTENT INVENTORY

Once you have a an idea of your Web site's mission and general structure, you can begin to assess the content you will need to realize your plans. Building an inventory or database of existing and needed content will force you to take a hard look at your existing content resources and to make a detailed outline of your needs. Once you know where you are short on content you can concentrate on those deficits and avoid wasting time on areas with existing resources that are ready to use. A clear grasp of your needs will also help you develop a realistic schedule and budget for the project. Content development is the hardest, most time-consuming part of any Web site development project. Starting early with a firm plan in hand will help ensure that you won't be caught later with a well-structured but empty Web site.

THE SITE DEVELOPMENT PROCESS

Every significant Web project poses unique challenges, but the overall process of developing a complex Web site generally follows six major stages:

1 Site definition and planning
2 Information architecture
3 Site design
4 Site construction
5 Site marketing
6 Tracking, evaluation, and maintenance

Developing a large Web site is a process that may have far-reaching budgetary, personnel, and public relations consequences for an organization, both during the development of the site and long after its successful deployment. Too many Web sites begin life as ad hoc efforts, created by small interest groups working in isolation from their peers elsewhere in the organization and without fully considering the site's goals within the context of the organization's overall mission. The result of poorly planned, hasty development efforts often is an "orphan site," starved of resources and attention.

As you consider the development process outlined below, note that the construction of the pages that make up the Web site is one of the *last* things that takes place in a well-designed project. Think before you act, and make sure you have the organizational backing, budget, and personnel resources you'll need to make the project a success.

I SITE DEFINITION AND PLANNING

This initial stage is where you define your goals and objectives for the Web site and begin to collect and analyze the information you'll need to justify the budget and resources required. This is also the time to define the scope of the site content, the interactive functionality and technology support required, and the depth and breadth of information resources that you will need to fill out the site and meet your reader's expectations. If you are contracting out the production of the Web site, you will also need to interview and select a site design firm. Ideally, your site designers should be involved as soon as possible in the planning discussions.

Production
- What are the purpose and goals for the site?
- Who is the target audience for the site, and what do they want?
- Will your site production team be composed of in-house people, outside contractors, or a mix of the two?
- Who will manage the process?
- Who are your primary content experts?
- Who will be the liaison to any outside contractors?
- Who will function long-term as the Webmaster or senior site editor?

Technology
- What browsers and operating systems should your site support?
    Windows, Macintosh, UNIX
    Netscape Navigator, Internet Explorer; minimum version supported
        (3.0, 4.0)
- Network bandwidth of average site visitors
    Internal audience or a largely external audience?
    Ethernet or high-speed connections
    Faster modem, ISDN (Integrated Services Digital Network), or DSL
        connections
    Typical modem connections
- Dynamic HTML (HyperText Markup Language) and advanced features
    Javascript or VBscript (Visual Basic Scripting Edition) required
    Java applets required
    Style sheets required
    Third-party browser plug-ins required
    Proprietary features of Netscape or Microsoft
    Special security features required
- How will readers reach the support personnel?
    Email messages from readers
    Chat rooms, forums
- Database support?
    User log-ins required to enter any site areas?
    Questionnaires required?
    Search and retrieval from databases needed?
- Audiovisual content
    Video or audio productions?

Web server support
- In-house Web server or outsourced to Internet Service Provider (ISP)?
    Unique domain names available (multihoming)
    Disk space or site traffic limitations or extra costs
    Adequate capacity to meet site traffic demands?
    Twenty-four-hour, seven-days-a-week support and maintenance?
    Statistics on users and site traffic?
    Server log analysis: in-house or outsourced?
    Search engine suitable for your content?
    CGI (Common Gateway Interface), programming, and database
        middleware support available?
    Database support or coordination with in-house staff?

Budgeting
- Salaries and benefits
- Hardware and software for in-house team members
- Staff training in Web use, database, Web marketing, and Web design
- Outsourcing fees
    Site design and development
    Technical consulting
    Database development
    Site marketing
- Ongoing personnel support for site
    Site editor or Webmaster
- Ongoing server and technical support
- Database maintenance and support
- New content development and updating

2 INFORMATION ARCHITECTURE

At this stage you need to detail the content and organization of the Web site. The team should inventory all existing content, describe what new content is required, and define the organizational structure of the site. Once a content architecture has been sketched out, you should build small prototypes of parts of the site to test what it feels like to move around within the design. Site prototypes are useful for two reasons. First, they are the best way to test site navigation and develop the user interface. The prototypes should incorporate enough pages to assess accurately what it's like to move from menus to content pages. Second, creating a prototype allows the graphic designers to develop relations between how the site looks and how the navigation interface supports the information design. The key to good prototyping is flexibility early on: the site prototypes should not be so complex or elaborate that the team becomes too invested in one design at the expense of exploring alternatives.

Typical results or contract deliverables at the end of this stage could include:

- Detailed site design specification
- Detailed description of site content
    Site maps, thumbnails, outlines, table of contents
- Detailed technical support specification
    Browser technology supported
    Connection speed supported
    Web server and server resources
- Proposals to create programming or technology to support specific features of the site
- A schedule for implementing the site design and construction
- One or more site prototypes of multiple pages
- Multiple graphic design and interface design sketches or roughs

3 SITE DESIGN

At this stage the project acquires its look and feel, as the page grid, page design, and overall graphic design standards are created and approved. Now the illustrations, photography, and other graphic or audiovisual content for the site need to be commissioned and created. Research, writing, organizing, assembling, and editing the site's text content is also performed at this stage. Any programming, database design and data entry, and search engine design should be well under way by now. The goal is to produce all the content components and functional programming and have them ready for the final production stage: the construction of the actual Web site pages.

Typical products or contract deliverables at the end of this stage could include:

Content components, detailed organization and assembly
- Text, edited and proofread
- Graphic design specifications for all page types
    Finished interface graphics for page templates
    Header and footer graphics, logos, buttons, backgrounds
- Detailed page comps or finished examples of key pages
    Site graphic standards manual for large, complex sites
- Interface design and master page grid templates completed
    Finished HTML template pages
- Illustrations
- Photography

Functional and logic components
- Javascript scripts, Java applets designed
- Database tables and programming, interaction prototypes completed
- Search engine designed and tested

4 SITE CONSTRUCTION

Only at this mature stage of the project are the bulk of the site's Web pages constructed and filled out with content. By waiting until you have a detailed site architecture, mature content components, and a polished page design specification you will minimize the content churning, redundant development efforts, and wasted energy that inevitably result from rushing to create pages too soon. Of course, you will always learn new things about your overall design as the prototype matures into the full-blown Web site. Be prepared to refine your designs as you navigate through the growing Web site and discover both weak spots and opportunities to improve navigation or content.

Once the site has been constructed, with all pages completed and all database and programming components linked, it is ready for beta testing. Testing should be done primarily by readers outside your site development team who are willing to supply informed criticism and report programming bugs, typographic errors, and critique the overall design and effectiveness of the site. Fresh users will inevitably notice things that you and your development team have overlooked. Only after the site has been thoroughly tested should you begin to publicize the URL (Uniform Resource Locator) address of the site to a larger audience.

Typical products or contract deliverables at the end of this stage should include:

- Finished HTML for all Web pages, all page content in place
- Finished navigation link structure
- All programming in place and linked to pages, ready for beta testing
- All database components in place and linked to site pages
- All graphic design, illustration, and photography in place
- Final proofreading of all site content
- Detailed testing of database and programming functionality
- Testing and verification of database reporting features
- Testing of site reader support procedures, answering email, etc.
- Archives of all site content components, HTML code, programming code, and any other site development materials

5 SITE MARKETING

Your Web site should be an integral part of all marketing campaigns and corporate communications programs, and the URL for your site should appear on every piece of correspondence and marketing collateral your organization generates.

If your Web site is aimed primarily at local audiences you must look beyond getting listed in standard Web indexes, such as Yahoo and Infoseek, URL and publicize your URL where local residents or businesses will encounter it. Local libraries (and schools, where the content is relevant) are often the key to publicizing a new Web site within a localized geographic area.

You may also find opportunities to cross-promote your site with affiliated businesses, professional organizations, broadcast or print media, visitor or local information agencies, real estate and relocation services, Internet access providers, and local city or town directory sites. Your organization could also feature local nonprofit charitable or school events on your Web site. The cost in server space is usually trivial, and highly publicized local events featuring a Web page hosted within your site will boost local awareness of your Web presence. Site sponsorship might also interest local broadcast media as an interesting story angle.

Your home page URL should appear in all:

- Print advertisements
- Radio and television advertisements
- Lobby kiosks in high-traffic areas of your enterprise or in local libraries, schools, or other suitable venues
- Direct mail campaigns
- Business cards
- Stationery
- Bills and statements
- Product manuals, product packaging
- Response cards, warrantee cards
- Publications and promotional materials
- Press releases
- Posters and billboards

6 TRACKING, EVALUATION, AND MAINTENANCE

An abundance of information about visitors to your site can be recorded with your Web server software. Even the simplest site logs track how many people (unique visitors) saw your site over a given time, how many pages were requested for viewing, and many other variables. By analyzing the server logs for your Web site you can develop quantitative data on the success of your site. The logs will tell you what pages were the most popular and what brands and versions of Web browser people used to view your site. Server logs can also give you information on the geographic location of your site readers. The usefulness of your site logs will depend on what you ask of the server and the people who maintain the server. Detailed logs are the key to quantifying the success of a Web site. Your Webmaster should archive all site logs for long-term analysis and should be prepared to add or change the information categories being logged as your needs and interests change.

You can also tease out more subtle information that can warn you of design problems with your site. If the "hits" (number of times the file was requested) on the graphics files used on your home page are significantly lower than the hits on the page HTML file itself, it's a good indication that many visitors are choosing not to load the page graphics (the page shows a hit when this happens, but the graphics files are untouched). This could be a warning that you have too many graphics on your page, or it could just be confirmation that many of your readers are using relatively slow modem connections to visit your site. (Modem users often choose not to view page graphics automatically as a way of speeding up Web surfing.) If the hit rate on a menu screen in part of your site is much higher than any of the pages linked from the menu, it could be an indication that readers do not find the menu attractive or useful. As you develop data on the usage of your site you can begin to refine the site, improving or eliminating site content that attracts few readers, and developing more of the content for sections that generate the greatest user response and site traffic.

Maintaining the site

Don't abandon your site once the production "goes public" and the parties are over. The aesthetic and functional aspects of a large Web site need constant attention and grooming, particularly if a group of individuals shares responsibility for updating content. Someone will need to be responsible for coordinating and vetting the new content stream, maintaining the graphic and editorial standards, and assuring that the programming and linkages of all pages remain intact and functional. Links on the Web are perishable, and you'll need to check periodically that links to pages outside your immediate site are still working. Don't let your site go stale by starving it of resources just as you begin to develop an audience – if you disappoint them by not following through it will be doubly difficult to attract them back.

2   *Interface Design*

I have an existential map. It has "you are here" written all over it.
– Steven Wright

USERS OF WEB DOCUMENTS don't just look at information, they interact with it in novel ways that have no precedents in paper document design. The graphic user interface (GUI) of a computer system comprises the interaction metaphors, images, and concepts used to convey function and meaning on the computer screen. It also includes the detailed visual characteristics of every component of the graphic interface and the functional sequence of interactions over time that produce the characteristic look and feel of Web pages and hypertext linked relations. Graphic design and visual "signature" graphics are not used simply to enliven Web pages – graphics are integral to the user's experience with your site. In interactive documents graphic design cannot be separated from issues of interface design.

WEB PAGE DESIGN VERSUS CONVENTIONAL DOCUMENT DESIGN
Concepts about structuring information today stem largely from the organization of printed books and periodicals and the library indexing and catalog systems that developed around printed information. The "interface standards" of books in the English-speaking world are well established and widely agreed-upon, and detailed instructions for creating books may be found in such guides as *The Chicago Manual of Style*. Every feature of the book, from the contents page to the index, has evolved over the centuries, and readers of early books faced some of the same organizational problems that users of hypermedia documents confront today. Gutenberg's Bible of 1456 is often cited as the first modern book, yet even after the explosive growth of publishing that followed Gutenberg's invention of printing with movable type, it was more than a century before page numbering, indexes, tables of contents, and even title pages became expected and necessary features of books. Web documents will undergo a similar evolution and standardization.

Design precedents in print   Although networked interactive hypermedia documents pose novel challenges to information designers, most of the guidance needed to design, create, assemble, edit, and organize multiple forms of media does not differ radically from current practice in print media. Most Web documents can be made to conform to *The Chicago Manual of Style* conventions for editorial style and text organization. Much of what an organization needs to know about creating clear, comprehensive, and consistent internal publishing standards is already available in such publishing guides as the *Xerox Publishing Standards: A Manual of Style and Design*. Don't get so lost in the novelty of Web pages that basic standards of editorial and graphic design are tossed aside.

MAKE YOUR WEB PAGES FREESTANDING

World Wide Web pages differ from books and other documents in one crucial respect: hypertext links allow users to access a single Web page with no preamble. For this reason Web pages need to be more independent than pages in a book. For example, the headers and footers of Web pages should be more informative and elaborate than those on printed pages. It would be absurd to repeat the copyright information, author, and date of a book at the bottom of every printed page, but individual Web pages often need to provide such information because a single Web page may be the only part of a site that some users will see. This problem of making documents freestanding is not unique to Web pages. Journals, magazines, and most newspapers repeat the date, volume number, and issue number at the top or bottom of each printed page because they know that readers often rip out articles or photocopy pages and will need that information to be able to trace the source of the material.

Given the difficulties inherent in creating Web sites that are both easy to use and full of complex content, the best design strategy is to apply a few fundamental document design principles consistently in every Web page you create. The basic elements of a document aren't complicated and have almost nothing to do with Internet technology. It's like a high school journalism class: who, what, when, and where.

Who Who is speaking? This question is so basic, and the information is so often taken for granted, that authors frequently overlook the most fundamental piece of information a reader needs to assess the provenance of a Web document. Whether the page originates from an individual author or an institution, always tell the reader who created it. The flood of Web sites propagating incorrect or intentionally misleading material on the crash of TWA Flight 800 in 1996 offers a vivid example of how "information" of no known origin and of dubious authenticity can quickly dominate legitimate inquiry and discussion.

What All documents need clear titles to capture the reader's attention, but for several reasons peculiar to the Web this basic editorial element is especially crucial. The document title is often the first thing browsers of World Wide Web documents see as the page comes up. In pages with lots of graphics the title may be the only thing the user sees for several seconds as the graphics download onto the page. In addition, the page title will become the text of a browser "bookmark" if the user chooses to add your page to his or her list of URLs. A misleading or ambiguous title or one that contains more technical gibberish than English will not help users remember why they bookmarked your page.

When Timeliness is an important element in evaluating the worth of a document. We take information about the age of most paper documents for granted: newspapers, magazines, and virtually all office correspondence is dated. Date every Web page, and change the date whenever the document is updated. This is especially important in long or complex online documents that are updated regularly but may not look different enough to signal a change in content to occasional readers. Corporate information, personnel manuals, product information, and other technical documents delivered as Web pages should always carry version numbers or revision dates. Remember that many readers prefer to print long documents from the Web. If you don't include revision dates your audience may not be able to assess whether the version they have in hand is current.

Where The Web is an odd "place" that has huge informational dimensions but few explicit cues to the place of origin of a document. Click on a Web link, and you could be connected to a Web server in Sydney, Australia, Chicago, or Rome – anywhere, in fact, with an Internet connection. Unless you are well versed in parsing URLs it can be hard to tell where a page originates. This is the World Wide Web, after all, and the question of where a document comes from is sometimes inseparable from whom the document comes from. Always tell the reader where you are from, with (if relevant) your corporate or institutional affiliations.

Incorporating the "home" URL on at least the main pages of your site is an easy way to maintain the connection to where a page originated. Once the reader has saved the page as a text file or printed the page onto paper, this connection may be lost. Although newer versions of the most common Web browsers allow users to include the URL automatically in anything they print, many people never take advantage of this optional feature. Too many of us have stacks of printed Web pages with no easy way of locating the Web sites where they originated.

Every Web page needs:
- An informative title
- The creator's identity (author or institution)
- A creation or revision date
- At least one link to a local home page
- The "home page" URL on the major menu pages in your site

Include these basic elements and you will have traveled 90 percent of the way toward providing your readers with an understandable Web user interface.

BASIC INTERFACE DESIGN

USER-CENTERED DESIGN

Graphic user interfaces were designed to give people control over their personal computers. Users now expect a level of design sophistication from all graphic interfaces, including Web pages. The goal is to provide for the needs of all your potential users, adapting Web technology to their expectations and never requiring readers to conform to an interface that places unnecessary obstacles in their paths.

This is where your research on the needs and demographics of the target audience is crucial. It's impossible to design for an unknown person whose needs you don't understand. Create sample scenarios with different types of users seeking information from your site. Would an experienced user seeking a specific piece of information be helped or hindered by your home page design? Would a novice be intimidated by a complex menu scheme? Testing your designs and getting feedback from a variety of users is the best way to see whether your design ideas are giving them what they want from your site.

Clear navigation aids   Most user interactions with Web pages involve navigating hypertext links between documents. The main interface problem in Web sites is the lack of a sense of where you are within the local organization of information:

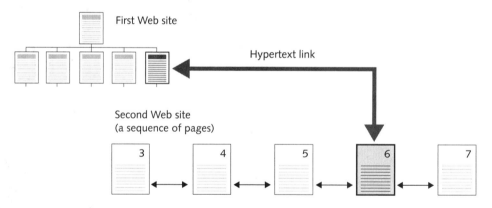

Clear, consistent icons, graphic identity schemes, and graphic or text-based overview and summary screens can give the user confidence that they can find what they are looking for without wasting time.

Users should always be able to return easily to your home page and to other major navigation points in the site. These basic links should be present on every page. Graphic buttons will provide basic navigation links and create a graphic identity that tells users they are within the site domain. In this academic medicine site, for example, the following graphic header appears on every page:

YALE-NEW HAVEN MEDICAL CENTER

| Home page | Search | ◀ | ▶ |

| Yale-New Haven Hospital | Yale School of Medicine | Yale School of Nursing | Epidemiology & Public Health |

| Find a physician | Find a person | Yale Medical Library | Academic departments | Calendar | Index |

The button bar is efficient (offering multiple choices in a small space) and predictable (it is always there, at the bottom of every page), and it provides a consistent graphic identity throughout the site.

No dead-end pages   Web pages often appear with no preamble: readers can make or follow links directly to subsection pages buried deep in the hierarchy of Web sites. They may never see your home page or other introductory site information. If your subsection pages do not contain links to the home page or to local menu pages, the reader will be locked out from the rest of the Web site:

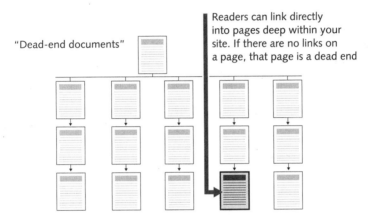

"Dead-end documents"

Readers can link directly into pages deep within your site. If there are no links on a page, that page is a dead end

Direct access   Users want to get information in the fewest possible steps. This means that you must design an efficient hierarchy of information to minimize steps through menu pages. Studies have shown that users prefer menus that present at least five to seven links and that they prefer a few very dense screens of choices to many layers of simplified menus. The following table demonstrates that you do not need many levels of menus to incorporate lots of choices:

	Number of menu items listed			
Number of nested menus	5	7	8	10
1	5	7	8	10
2	25	49	64	100
3	125	343	512	1000

Bandwidth and interaction   Users will not tolerate long delays. Research has shown that for most computing tasks the threshold of frustration is about ten seconds. Web page designs that are not well "tuned" to the network access speed of typical users will only frustrate them. If your users are primarily general public browsers "surfing" the Web via modem connections it is foolish to put huge bitmap graphics on your pages – the average user will not be patient enough to wait while your graphics download over the phone line. If, however, you are building a university or corporate intranet site where most users will access the Web server at Ethernet speeds or better, you can be much more ambitious in the use of graphics and multimedia.

Simplicity and consistency   Users are not impressed with complexity that seems gratuitous, especially those who may be depending on the site for timely and accurate work-related information. Your interface metaphors should be simple, familiar, and logical – if you need a metaphor for information design, choose a book or a library, not a spacecraft or a television set. The best information designs are the ones most users never notice. Studio Archetype's work for the Adobe Corporation Web site is an excellent model of interface design. Graphic headers act as navigation aids and are consistently applied across every page in the site. Once you know where the standard links are on the page header graphics, the interface becomes almost invisible and navigation is easy:

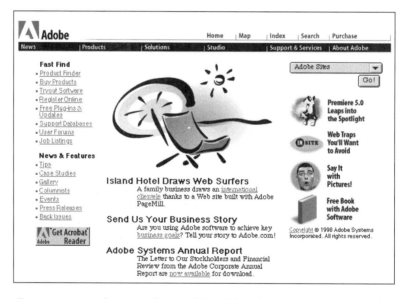

For maximum functionality and legibility, your page and site design should be built on a consistent pattern of modular units that all share the same basic layout grids, graphic themes, editorial conventions, and hierarchies of organization. The goal is to be consistent and predictable; your users should feel comfortable exploring your site and confident that they can find what they need. The graphic identity of a series of pages in a Web site provides visual cues to the continuity of information. The header menu graphics present on every page of the Adobe site create a consistent user interface and corporate identity:

Even if your site design does not employ navigation graphics, a consistent approach to the layout of titles, subtitles, page footers, and navigation links to your home page or related pages will reinforce the reader's sense of context within the site. To preserve the effect of a "seamless" system of pages you may wish to bring important information into your site and adapt it to your page layout scheme rather than using links to send the reader away from your site (be sure there are no copyright restrictions on copying the information into your site).

Design integrity and stability   To convince your users that what you have to offer is accurate and reliable, you will need to design your Web site as carefully as you would any other type of corporate communication, using the same high editorial and design standards. A site that looks sloppily built, with poor visual design and low editorial standards, will not inspire confidence.

Functional stability in any Web design means keeping the interactive elements of the site working reliably. Functional stability has two components: getting things right the first time as you design the site, and then keeping things functioning smoothly over time. Good Web sites are inherently interactive, with lots of links to local pages within the site as well as links to other sites on the Web. As you create your design you will need to check frequently that all of your links work properly. Information changes quickly on the Web, both in your site and in everyone else's. After the site is established you will need to check that your links are still working properly and that the content they supply remains relevant.

Feedback and dialog   Your Web design should offer constant visual and functional confirmation of the user's whereabouts and options, via graphic design, navigation buttons, or uniformly placed hypertext links. Feedback also means being prepared to respond to your users' inquiries and comments. Well-designed Web sites provide direct links to the site's editor or "Webmaster" responsible for running the site. Planning for this ongoing relationship with users of your site is vital to the long-term success of the enterprise.

Disabled users   Not every user of your site will be able to take advantage of the graphics you offer on your pages, and a number of users may be visually impaired. One of the beauties of the Web and HTML is the ability to build in "alternate" messages (ALT tags in HTML) so that users without graphics capabilities can still understand the function of graphics on your pages. Using specially designed software, blind users can hear (via synthesized speech) the alternate messages you supply along with your graphics and so will not completely miss the content of your pictures and graphic navigation buttons. If you will be using graphic menu systems for navigation, these text-based alternate menus will be an especially important aid to users who lack the ability to see your graphics. If you use graphics such as single-pixel GIFs as spacers in your page layout, always be sure to include a blank ALT statement in the spacer image source tag (ALT=""). The blank ALT statement hides the graphic from text-only browsers and from browsers that read text aloud for visually impaired users:

```
<IMG SRC="pixel.gif" HEIGHT="1" WIDTH ="1" ALT="" HSPACE="5">
```

Graceful degradation We all hope that every reader will arrive using the latest version of a major Web browser and that their computers will be state-of-the art models using fast connections to the Internet. The reality is almost always less than ideal. You don't need to design your Web site exclusively for the lowest common denominator of current computing and network technology, but you do need to consider what your site will look like to those readers who do not have the best equipment, current software, and good Internet connections. The problems here are aggravated by the fact that Web site developers generally have much better equipment than the average Web site reader. Don't design for *your* machine, design for your average reader.

Always check your page designs on small screens (640 × 480 pixels), and on screens that display only 256 colors (8-bit displays). Many users with slow modem connections routinely turn off the image display in their browser. Try turning off graphics in your Web browser and look at your pages – are they still intelligible and navigable? Do you use ALT statements for every graphic? Do you use blank ALT statements (ALT="") to hide irrelevant graphics or spacer graphics from text-only browsers?

Do not produce Web sites that depend on one browser technology or browser plug-in ("This site designed for Netscape 4.05, and ShockWave"). Such notes on the home page of a corporate or enterprise Web site look sophomoric and will drive away most users old enough to drive. Design for everyone using major browsers released in the two previous years. If you must depend on proprietary browser plug-ins, try to position the material that is dependent on the plug-in deeper within the site, where presumably the reader will have already made a commitment to your content and may not mind the bother of having to download a plug-in to see special features. Once readers have a clearer sense of what they might gain by bothering to download a browser plug-in, they can make an informed decision.

NAVIGATION

A rich set of graphic navigation and interactivity links within your Web pages will pull users' attention down the page, weaning them from the general-purpose browser links and drawing them further into your content. By providing your own consistent and predictable set of navigation buttons you also give the user a sense of your site's organization and make the logic and order of your site visually explicit. Here the rich graphics and many links offered by the "Nova" home page immediately draw the reader into the site:

Provide context or lose the reader Readers need a sense of context, of their place within an organization of information. In paper documents this sense of "where you are" is a mixture of graphic and editorial organizational cues supplied by the graphic design of the book, the organization of the text, and the physical sensation of the book as an object. Electronic documents provide none of the physical cues we take for granted in assessing information. When we see a Web hypertext link on the page we have few cues to where we will be led, how much information is at the other end of the link, and exactly how the linked information relates to the current page. Even the view of individual Web pages is restricted for many users. Most Web pages don't fit completely on an standard office fourteen-inch or fifteen-inch display monitor, and so there is almost always a part of the page that the user cannot see:

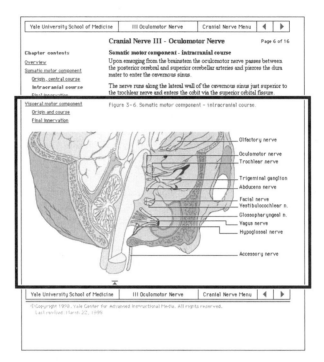

Web pages need to give the user explicit cues to the context and organization of information because only a small portion of any site (less than a page) is visible at one time:

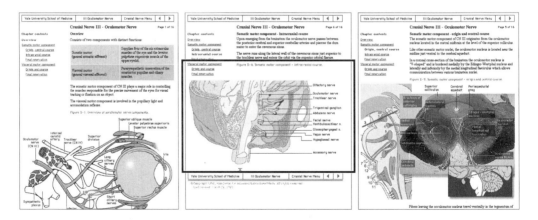

As the Web page designer it is up to you to provide these functional and context cues.

"Going back" and going to the previous page   All hypertext systems share a common feature that has no direct precedent in print media: going "back" through a series of links you have previously visited is not the same as paging "back" through the preceding pages of an ordered sequence of pages. When users click on a hypertext link in a Web document they often are transported from one Web site to another, perhaps even from one country to another. Once made, the hypertext link is bidirectional; you can "go back" to the Web site you just left by clicking on the "Back" button of the viewer. Having hit the "Back" button, you can move to the new Web site again by hitting the "Forward" button:

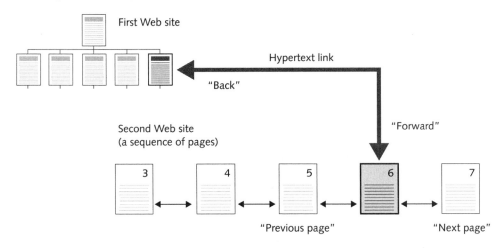

Why button bars are useful   For the information designer hypertext links are a mixed blessing. The radical shifts in context that links create can easily confuse Web users, who need organized cues and interface elements if they are to follow and understand hypertext links from one Web page to another. This is particularly true when users need to be able to follow (or at least recognize) an ordered sequence of documents. Notice in the diagram above that although the user has entered the second Web site at page 6, the site is an ordered sequence of pages.

If the standard Web viewer "Back" and "Forward" buttons are augmented with "Next Page" and "Previous Page" buttons built into the page, the user will have interface tools to navigate through the information in your site in the sequence you intended. Button bars can also display location information much the way running chapter headers do in printed books:

| Yale University School of Medicine | III Oculomotor Nerve | Cranial Nerve Menu | ◀ | ▶ |

Fixed versus relative links   Unlike the "Back" and "Forward" buttons in such Web viewers as Netscape Navigator and Microsoft Internet Explorer, whose functions are relative only to the pages you have seen most recently, "Next Page" and "Previous Page" buttons in a document are fixed links you provide to associated documents. By providing paging buttons and links to local home pages and contents pages you give users the tools to understand how you have organized your Web site information, even if they have not entered your web of pages through a home page or contents page. The buttons don't prevent people from reading the information in whatever order they choose, but they do allow readers to follow the sequence of pages you have laid out:

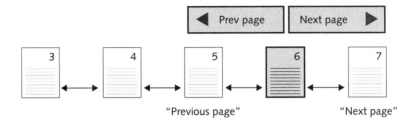

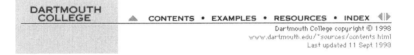

Button bars are also the most logical place for links back to your home page or to other menu pages related to the current page. A button bar can be built with text-based links or a series of individual button graphics at the top or bottom of the page:

3 Site Design

Find out what they like, and how they like it,
And let 'em have it just that way.
– Fats Waller

THE DESIGN OF THE SITE will determine its organizational framework. At this stage you will make the essential decisions about what your audience wants from you, what you wish to say, and how to arrange the content to best meet your audience's needs. Although people will notice the graphic design of your Web pages right away, the organization of the site will have the greatest impact on their experience.

The fundamental organizing principle in Web site design is meeting users' needs. Ask yourself what your audience wants, and center your site design around their needs. Many organizations and businesses make the mistake of using their Web sites primarily to describe their administrative organization, and only secondarily do they offer the services, products, and information the average user is seeking. Most readers won't care how your company or department is organized and will be put off if such inside information is all your site appears to offer. Talk to the people who make up your target audience, put yourself in their shoes, and make the items and services they want the most prominent items on the home page.

Notice, in the illustration below, how the major categories in the Yale–New Haven Hospital home page center on the needs and interests of various audiences, not on how the hospital is organized:

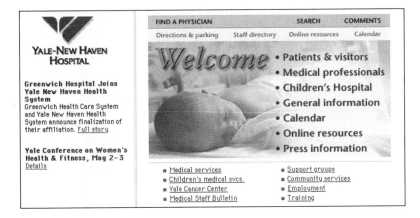

ORGANIZING INFORMATION

Our day-to-day professional and social lives rarely demand that we create detailed architectures of what we know and how those structures of information are linked. Yet without a solid and logical organizational foundation, your Web site will not function well even if your basic content is accurate, attractive, and well written. Cognitive psychologists have known for decades that most people can hold only about four to seven discrete chunks of information in short-term memory. The way people seek and use reference information also suggests that smaller, discrete units of information are more functional and easier to handle than long, undifferentiated tracts.

There are five basic steps in organizing your information:

1 Divide your content into logical units
2 Establish a hierarchy of importance among the units
3 Use the hierarchy to structure relations among units
4 Build a site that closely follows your information structure
5 Analyze the functional and aesthetic success of your system

"CHUNKING" INFORMATION

Most information on the World Wide Web is gathered in short reference documents that are intended to be read nonsequentially. This is particularly true of sites whose contents are mostly technical or administrative documents. Long before the Web was invented, technical writers discovered that readers appreciate short "chunks" of information that can be located and scanned quickly. This method for presenting information translates well to the Web for several reasons:

- Few Web users spend time reading long passages of text on-screen. Most users either save long documents to disk or print them out.
- Discrete chunks of information lend themselves to Web links. The user of a Web link usually expects to find a specific unit of relevant information, not a book's worth of content. But don't over-subdivide your information or you will frustrate your readers. One to two pages (as printed) of information is about the maximum size for a discrete chunk of information on the Web.
- Chunking can help organize and present information in a uniform format. This allows users both to apply their past experience with a site to future searches and explorations and to predict how an unfamiliar section of a Web site will be organized.
- Concise chunks of information are better suited to the computer screen, which provides a limited view of long documents. Long Web pages tend to disorient readers; they require users to scroll long distances and to remember what is off-screen.

The concept of a chunk of information must be flexible and consistent with common sense, logical organization, and convenience. Let the nature of the content suggest how it should be subdivided and organized. At times it makes sense to provide long documents as a subdivided and linked set of Web pages. Although short Web documents are usually preferable, it makes little sense to divide up a long document arbitrarily, particularly if you want users to be able to print easily or save the entire document in one step.

Hierarchy of importance   Hierarchical organization is virtually a necessity on the Web. Most sites depend on hierarchies, moving from the most general overview of the site (the home page), down through increasingly specific submenus and content pages. Chunks of information should be ranked in importance and organized by the interrelations among units. Once you have determined a logical set of priorities, you can build a hierarchy from the most important or general concepts down to the most specific or detailed topics.

Relations   When confronted with a new and complex information system, users build mental models. They use these models to assess relations among topics and to guess where to find things they haven't seen before. The success of the organization of your Web site will be determined largely by how well your system matches your users' expectations. A logical site organization allows users to make successful predictions about where to find things. Consistent methods of displaying information permit users to extend their knowledge from familiar pages to unfamiliar ones. If you mislead users with a structure that is neither logical nor predictable, they will be frustrated by the difficulties of getting around. You don't want your users' mental model of your Web site to look like this:

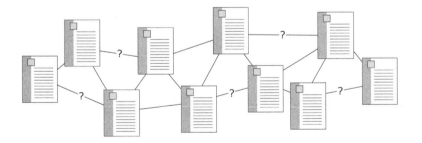

Function   Once you have created your site, analyze its functionality. Efficient Web site design is largely a matter of balancing the relation of menu, or home, pages with individual content pages. The goal is to build a hierarchy of menus and pages that feels natural to users and doesn't mislead them or interfere with their use of the site.

Web sites with too shallow a hierarchy depend on massive menu pages that can degenerate into a confusing "laundry list" of unrelated information:

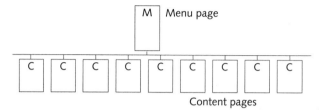

Menu schemes can also be too deep, burying information beneath too many layers of menus. Having to navigate through layers of nested menus before reaching real content is frustrating:

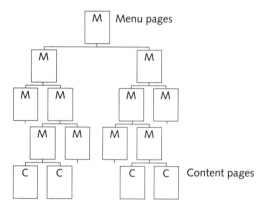

If your Web site is actively growing, the proper balance of menus and content pages is a moving target. Feedback from users (and analyzing your own use of the site) can help you decide if your menu scheme has outlived its usefulness or has weak areas. Complex document structures require deeper menu hierarchies, but users should never be forced into page after page of menus if direct access is possible. With a well-balanced, functional hierarchy you can offer users menus that provide quick access to information and reflect the organization of your site.

SUMMARY

The most important step in planning your site is organizing your information. Thinking carefully about what you want to say and how you want to say it requires that you become intimately acquainted with your site content. Create outlines, chunk your information into sections and subsections, think about how the sections relate to one another, and create a table of contents. This exercise will help immensely when it comes time to build the individual pages of your site and may determine the eventual success of your Web site.

A well-organized table of contents can be a major navigation tool in your Web site. The table is more than a list of links – it gives the user an overview of the organization, extent, and narrative flow of your presentation:

Yale C/AIM Web Style Guide

Patrick J. Lynch
Yale Center for Advanced Instructional Media

Sarah Horton
Dartmouth Curricular Computing
Dartmouth Didactic Web

Search this site:

[Search]

Detailed search page

Philosophy
Introduction
Purpose of the site
Design strategies

Interface Design
Introduction
Basic interface design for the Web
Information access issues
Navigation
Links & navigation

Site Design
Introduction
Site structure
Site elements I
Site elements II
Intranet design factors
Site Covers

Page Design
Introduction
Graphic design 100
Balanced pages & menus
Design grids for pages
Graphic safe areas for Web pages
Page headers & footers
Typography I
Typography II
Typefaces
Consistency

SITE STRUCTURE

If you are interested in the World Wide Web you can hardly escape references to hypertext and hypermedia. The computer press is full of fuzzy thinking about how Web-based information can somehow "link everything to everything." The implication is that with the Web you can dispense with one of the most challenging aspects of presenting information – putting it into a logical order and creating an interesting and understandable resource for readers. But if your idea of how one section of your site relates to other areas is hazy, if you have no comprehensive narrative or clear sense of organization, your readers will know it soon enough, and most will leave in pursuit of better material.

BASIC INFORMATION STRUCTURES

Web sites are built around basic structural themes. These fundamental architectures govern the navigational interface of the Web site and mold the user's mental models of how the information is organized. Four essential structures can be used to build a Web site: sequences, grids, hierarchies, and webs.

Sequences   The simplest way to organize information is to place it in a sequence. Sequential ordering may be chronological, a logical series of topics progressing from the general to the specific, or alphabetical, as in indexes, encyclopedias, and glossaries. Straight sequences are the most appropriate organization for training sites, for example, in which the reader is expected to go through a fixed set of material and the only links are those that support the linear path:

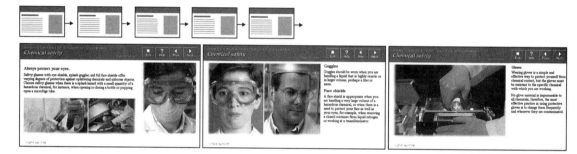

More complex Web sites may still be organized as a logical sequence, but each page in the main sequence may have links to one or more pages of digressions, parenthetical information, or information on other Web sites:

Grids   Many procedural manuals, lists of university courses, and medical case descriptions are best organized as a grid. Grids are a good way to correlate variables, such as a timeline versus historical information in a number of standard categories such as "events," "technology," and "culture." To be successful, the individual units in a grid must share a highly uniform structure of topics and subtopics, and the audience must understand the nature of the overall structure. Grid topics often have no particular hierarchy of importance. "Tuberculosis," for example, is no more or less important a diagnosis than "hilar adenopathy," but ideally both case descriptions would share a uniform structure of subtopics. Thus the user could follow the grid "down," reading about tuberculosis, or cut "across" the grid perhaps by comparing the "diagnostic imaging" sections of both hilar adenopathy and tuberculosis. Web-enabled databases are ideal for organizing the content of grid-structured Web sites because well-designed database records are inherently uniform in structure.

Unfortunately, grids can be hard to follow unless users recognize the interrelations among categories of information. For this reason, grids are probably best suited for experienced audiences with some understanding of the topic and its logical organization. Graphic overview maps are very useful in gridlike Web sites to communicate the structure of the grid and make users aware of their navigation options.

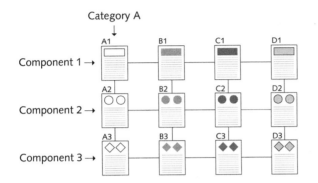

Hierarchies Information hierarchies are the best way to organize most complex bodies of information. Because Web sites are usually organized around a single home page, hierarchical schemes are particularly suited to Web site organization. Hierarchical diagrams are very familiar in corporate and institutional life, so most users find this structure easy to understand. A hierarchical organization also imposes a useful discipline on your own analytical approach to your content, because hierarchies are practical only with well-organized material.

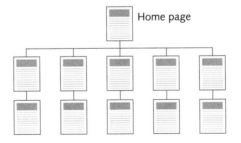

Webs Weblike organizational structures pose few restrictions on the pattern of information use. In this structure the goal is often to mimic associative thought and the free flow of ideas, allowing users follow their interests in a unique, heuristic, idiosyncratic pattern. This organizational pattern develops with dense links both to information elsewhere in the site and to information at other sites. Although the goal of this organization is to exploit the Web's power of linkage and association to the fullest, weblike structures can just as easily propagate confusion. Ironically, associative organizational schemes are often the most impractical structure for Web sites because they are so hard for the user to understand and predict. Webs work best for small sites dominated by lists of links and for sites aimed at highly educated or experienced users looking for further education or enrichment and not for a basic understanding of a topic.

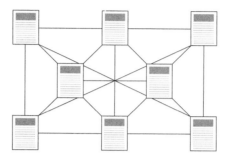

Summary   Most complex Web sites share aspects of all four types of information structures. Except in sites that rigorously enforce a sequence of pages, users are likely to use your site in a free-form weblike manner, just as they would a reference book. But the nonlinear usage patterns typical of Web surfers do not absolve you of the need to organize your thinking and present it within a clear, consistent structure that complements your design goals. The chart below summarizes the four basic organization patterns against the "linearity" of the narrative and the complexity of the content:

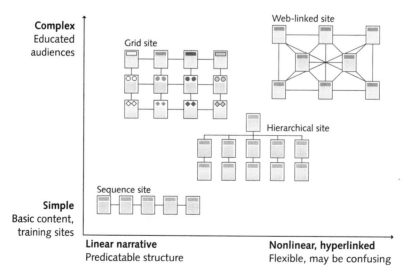

SITE DESIGN THEMES

All presentations of information are governed by parameters determined by the objectives, the practical logistics of the chosen medium, and the audience. The figure below plots four major themes for information delivery against two fundamental variables: the linearity of the structure of your presentation and the length of the typical user's contact time:

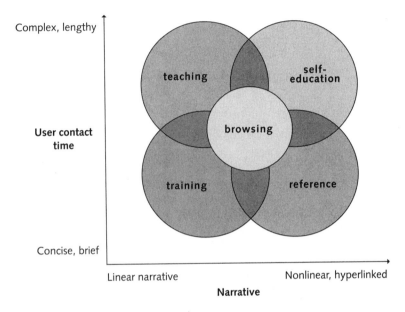

The following categories of Web use – training, teaching, continuing education, and reference – are typical of corporate and educational intranet sites in which readers arrive with a defined purpose.

Training Web-based training applications tend to be linear in design and typically present few opportunities to digress from the central flow of the presentation. Don't confuse readers or confound your own expectations by offering many links away from the central message. Restricting links to the "Next" and "Previous" paging functions guarantees that everyone will see the same core presentation and allows you to predict users' contact time more accurately. Most training presentations assume a contact time of less than one hour or are broken up into sessions of an hour or less. Tell your readers how long the session will last, and warn them not to digress from the required material if they are to receive credit for the training. Training applications typically require a user log-in and often present forms-based quiz questions in true-false or multiple-choice formats. User registration data and scores are typically stored in a database linked to the Web site.

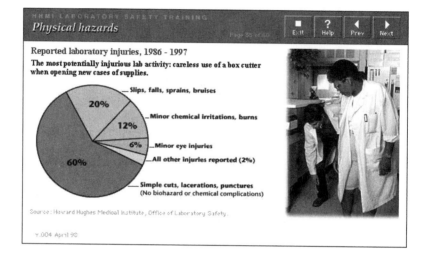

Teaching Good teaching applications are also built around a strong central narrative, but they typically offer more opportunities to pursue interesting digressions from the main themes of the Web site. The information presented is usually more sophisticated and in-depth than in training applications. Links are the most powerful aspect of the Web, but they can also be a distraction that may prevent visitors from getting through the presentation. If you wish to provide links to other Web-based resources beyond your local site, you might consider grouping the links on a separate page away from the main body of the material. Often readers will want to print material from a teaching site and read it later from paper. Make this easy for them by providing a "printing" version that consolidates many separate pages into one long page.

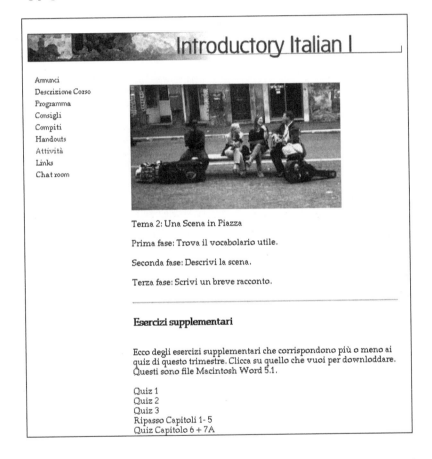

Continuing education The audiences for heuristic, self-directed learning will chafe at design strategies that are too restrictive or linear. The typical corporate or academic user of such sites is usually fairly knowledgeable in the subject area. Flexible, interactive, nonlinear design structures are ideal for these readers because it is difficult to predict exactly which topics will most interest them. The design must permit fast access to a wide range of topics and is typically dense with links to related material within the local site and beyond on the World Wide Web. Text-based lists of links work well here for tables of contents and indexes because they load fast and are full of information, but well-designed graphics and illustrations are also needed so that this easily bored audience will stay involved with the material. Contact times are unpredictable but are often shorter than for training or teaching sites because the readers are usually under time pressure. Easy printing options are another must for this audience.

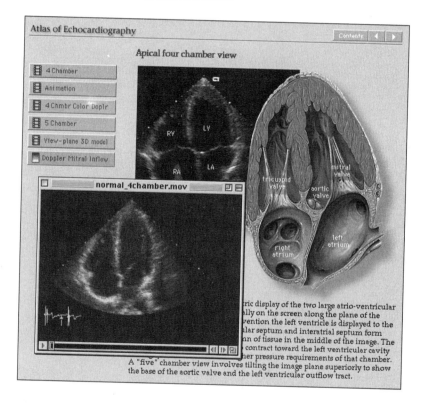

Reference The best-designed reference Web sites allow readers to pop into the site, find what they want, and easily print or download what they find. There is typically no "story" to tell, so usage patterns are nonlinear. Graphics should be minimal, and content and menu structure must be carefully organized to support fast search and retrieval, easy downloading of files, and convenient printing options. A well-designed search engine is a must for sites with more than thirty to fifty pages or sites that store long text documents in single Web pages. You may wish to investigate more sophisticated multiparameter search software instead of relying on single keyword searches. Contact time is typically brief in reference sites: the shorter the better.

Cushing/Whitney Medical Library
Selected Internet Resources in Biomedicine

What's New! The most recent 50 additions to the SIR database

DISCIPLINES & DISEASES	GENERAL RESOURCES	CONSUMER HEALTH
AIDS/HIV	Atlases	General Health Resources
Allergy and Immunology	Biographical Resources	Consumer Health Databases
Anatomy	Clinical Guidelines	AIDS
Anesthesiology	Clinical Trials	Allergy and Asthma
Basic Sciences	Continuing Education	Alzheimer's Disease
Bioethics	Databases	Arthritis
Biostatistics	Dictionaries	Breastfeeding
Cardiovascular Medicine	Directories	Cancer
Comparative Medicine	Discussion Groups	Children's Health
Critical Care	Drug Information	Depression
Dermatology	Education Resources	Diabetes
Diabetes	Employment	Diet and Nutrition
Dentistry	Encyclopedias	Digestive Diseases
Emergency Medicine	Equipment and Supply Catalogs	Fitness and Exercise
Endocrinology	Evidence-Based Medicine	Headache
Environmental Health	General Subject Guides	Heart Disease and Stroke
Epidemiology	Government Agencies	Integrative Medicine
Gastroenterology	Grants and Funding	Lyme Disease
Geriatrics	Handbooks	Men's Health
Health Policy	Images	Parenting
Hematology	Journals	Pregnancy and Childbirth
History of Science and Medicine	Laws and Regulations	Prescription Drug Information
Infectious Diseases	Libraries	Women's Health
International Health	Meetings and Conferences	
Medical Informatics	News Sources	
Neonatology	Nomenclature	
Nephrology	Organizations and Associations	
Neurology	Patents and Trademarks	
Neurosciences	Phone Books	
Neurosurgery	Quotations	
Nursing	Schools	
Obstetrics and Gynecology	Statistics	
Occupational Medicine	Tests and Measures	
Oncology	Texts	

SITE ELEMENTS

Web sites vary enormously in their style, content, organization, and purpose, but all Web sites that are designed primarily to act as information resources share certain characteristics.

HOME PAGES

All Web sites are organized around a home page that acts as a logical point of entry into the system of Web pages in a site. In hierarchical organizations, the home page sits at the top of the chart, and all pages in the Web site should contain a direct link back to the home page. The World Wide Web URL for a home page is the Web "address" that points users to the Web site. Home page addresses are rapidly becoming as important as home and business street addresses.

The thirty square inches at the top of a home page are the most visible area of the Web site. Most readers will be looking at your site on a thirteen- to fifteen-inch monitor, and the top four vertical inches are all that is sure to be visible on their screens. The best visual metaphor here is to a newspaper page – position matters. It's nice to be on the front page, but stories "above the fold" are much more visible than those below. In sites designed for efficient navigation the density of links at the top of the home page should be maximal – you'll never get a better chance to offer your readers exactly what they want in the first page they see:

"Above the fold" area is visible even on small screens

Most users will have to scroll to see these areas

Home pages perform a variety of functions. Some designs primarily take advantage of the high visibility of the home page; it's the most visited page of your site and is therefore ideal for posting news and information. The high visibility of the home page also makes it the ideal place to put a menu of links or table of contents for the site. Navigation schemes in sites that use the home page for news and menu listings are often centered around the home page, using it as the "home base" for most navigation through the site. Other home page designs use the home page as the first opportunity to steer audiences into subtopic or special-interest areas of the site. The following are the most common home page design strategies:

Menu home pages   Menu-like lists of links dominated the design of most home pages in the first few years of the Web, and this remains the most common type of home page. Menu-style pages need not be dominated by plain lists of text-based HTML links – graphic imagemaps are often more space efficient, packing the maximal number of links into every square inch of the page. Sophisticated designs combine graphic imagemaps and blocks of text-based links. Text links offer less visual impact but are much easier to change on short notice.

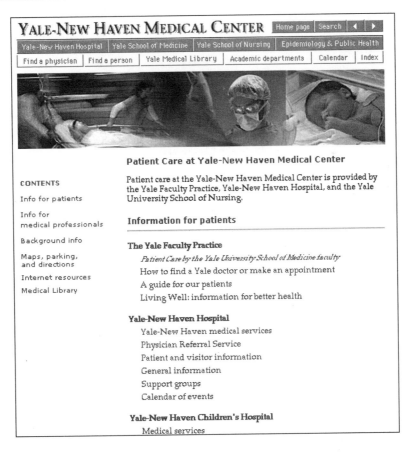

News-oriented home pages The home pages of such organizations as the *New York Times* and cnn (Cable News Network) are obvious examples here, but many organizations take advantage of the high visibility of their home pages to make announcements to both employees and the larger Web audience. Live information makes a home page more attractive and more likely to generate repeat visits. Many home page designs reserve one or more areas for late-breaking news, calendar events, or alert messages. If you choose this approach, standardize the location and nature of the news areas within a general page framework that remains stable over time. Readers will be disoriented if your home page changes too much from week to week.

Path-based home pages   Large Web sites offer so much information to so many audiences that it can be impossible to represent the depth and breadth of the site content in a single home page. In addition, readers often come to a Web site with specific interests or goals in mind. In such cases it is often advantageous to use the home page to split the audience immediately into interest groups and to offer them specific, more relevant information in menu pages deeper within the site.

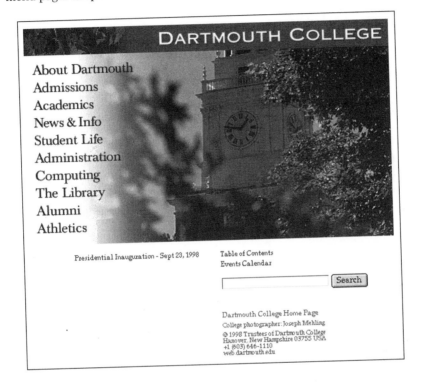

Splash screens   Splash screens, or site covers, are the most controversial of all site elements. For many readers, site covers are simply an additional and annoying mouse click between them and the content they are seeking. Such readers would like to be presented with a site index at the start rather than a splash screen with pretty graphics or spiffy animations. The key is to assess your audience and then choose the entry that seems most appropriate.

Consider the function of your site. Is your typical visitor there for a single visit or will they visit often? An online tool such as a calendar or search engine should not have a purely aesthetic site cover, because visitors may visit the site several times a day. An elegant but nonfunctional cover on such a site will soon become tedious. Of course, visitors who do not wish to enter through the front door can simply bookmark an internal page of your site, such as the table of contents. But if you find yourself repeatedly making this argument *for* using a splash screen, you may wish to adapt or even remove your cover to better accommodate your audience.

The success of splash screens depends enormously on the expectations of the site visitor. If you were to visit a site about a poet you would enter with different expectations than you would when visiting a site about carpal tunnel syndrome. Visitors to a site about poetry may not simply be out Web foraging but may instead be looking for an experience, for art, for entertainment. A mysterious, enigmatic, aesthetically pleasing facade might just entice such visitors in.

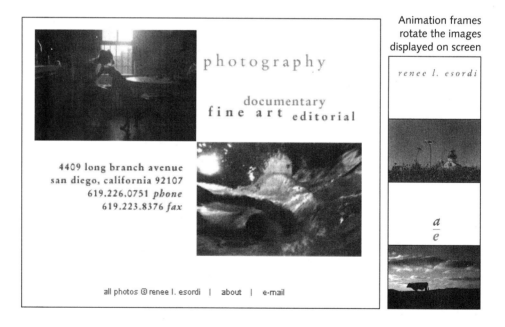

Animation frames rotate the images displayed on screen

One of these basic schemes may dominate the home page design, but increasingly home pages are a complex amalgam of all four strategies. Yale–New Haven Hospital's home page mixes a splash screen, menu listing, and news-oriented section while splitting users into such interest groups as "patients and visitors" and "medical professionals":

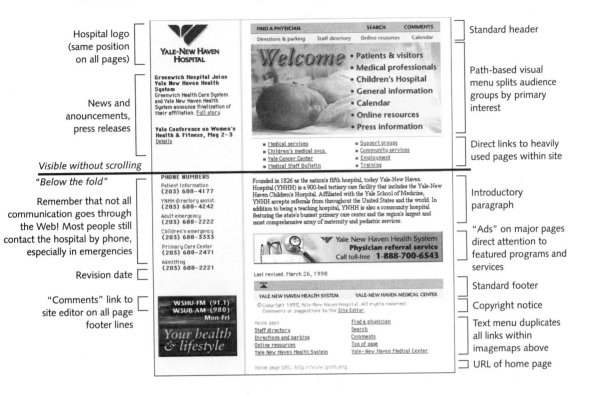

Hospital logo (same position on all pages)

News and anouncements, press releases

Visible without scrolling

"Below the fold"

Remember that not all communication goes through the Web! Most people still contact the hospital by phone, especially in emergencies

Revision date

"Comments" link to site editor on all page footer lines

Standard header

Path-based visual menu splits audience groups by primary interest

Direct links to heavily used pages within site

Introductory paragraph

"Ads" on major pages direct attention to featured programs and services

Standard footer

Copyright notice

Text menu duplicates all links within imagemaps above

URL of home page

Graphics or text?   The primary layout decision you will make about your home page is how heavily you will use graphics on the page. Most corporate, institutional, and education home pages display at least a small graphic banner across the top of the home page, and in commercial sites the trend is rapidly moving toward complex mixtures of links embedded in graphic imagemaps and links in text that emulate the look and functions of CD-ROM multimedia title pages or print magazines. Although strong graphics can be effective at grabbing a browser's attention, large graphic menus impose long loading times for pages, especially for users linking to the Internet via modems or slow network connections. Even if the user is accessing your Web site at Ethernet speeds, graphic menus may still load many times slower than text-based lists of links.

This dichotomy between slow-loading but attractive graphics-based home pages and fast-loading but prosaic text-based home pages also reflects the need to address multiple audiences with different expectations. The goals for most Web sites are to transmit internal information (to students, employees, and clients) and to communicate with potential clients and the general Web-browsing public. The Eastman Kodak Company has opted for graphic home page design, but the layout is carefully designed not to exceed the dimensions of the average office monitor. Because the graphic area is moderately sized, the page loads reasonably quickly for a graphic menu:

The relatively plain, mostly text-based home page for the World Wide Web Consortium offers a very efficient ratio of links per kilobyte of page size, but at some cost in pure visual appeal. The page is fast-loading and well designed for its audience of Web specialists but would not attract the average browser through presentation alone:

The best way to meet the needs of both casual browsers and highly targeted frequent users is to present alternative views of your Web site. One approach is to make a visually attractive main home page aimed at the general audience of Web browsers but also to offer a more text-oriented alternate home page that emphasizes rapid access to information via detailed text menus. Another approach is to use a graphic banner at the top of the home page, followed by a dense set of text-based links. The Library of Congress's congressional information Web site, "Thomas," reflects this dual approach, with a moderate-sized graphic image topping a dense but well-organized set of text links:

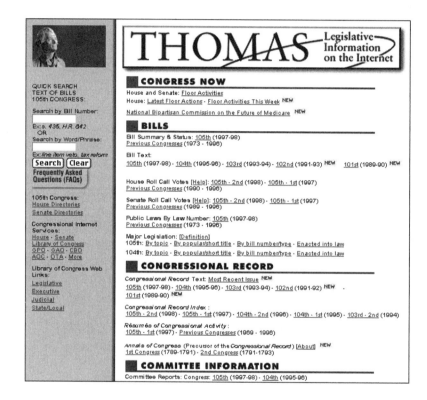

Many Web users who access the Internet via modems choose not to load graphics and thus will not see menu links embedded in imagemap graphics. If you choose to depend on links embedded in imagemaps, it is crucial to provide alternative text-based links that will remain visible even if readers have chosen to turn off the display of graphics. Many sites provide these text-based links in small sizes below the page footer, where they are accessible but do not disrupt the overall design of the page:

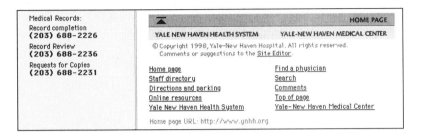

The master page layout grid The home page usually gets the most attention in the beginning of a Web site design project. Your home page is important, but remember – it is inherently singular. Don't let the design of the home page dominate your site design strategies. When designing a large Web site it's much more important to concentrate on the standard layout grid that *all* the internal pages of the site will share. After all, you'll have only one home page, but you could soon easily have thousands of internal pages. The overall success of the Web site will depend more on a strong, logical page grid than on the appeal of the site's home page. The details of page layout grids are discussed in the following chapters, but we raise the issue of page grids here because it is a crucial design decision when creating a Web site. Think about it: if you tire of your home page, you have only one page to change. Make a big mistake with your page grid and you could end up with thousands of poorly designed pages.

MENUS AND SUBSITES

Unless your site is small you will probably need a number of submenu pages that users enter from a general category listing on your home page. In complex sites with multiple topic areas it is not practical to burden the home page with dozens of links – the page grows too long to load in a timely manner, and its sheer complexity may be off-putting to many users. Providing a submenu page for each topic will create a mini-home page for each section of the site. For specialized, detailed submenus you could even encourage frequent users to link there directly. In this way the submenus will become alternate home pages in "subsites" oriented to a specific audience. Be sure to include a basic set of links to other sections of the site on each subsite home page, and always include a link back to your main organization home page.

RESOURCE LISTS, "OTHER RELATED SITES" PAGES

The World Wide Web is growing so rapidly that even the large commercial Web index services such as Yahoo and Excite are only partial listings of the information accessible through the Web. When authors begin to build Web sites, their first page is often a collection of favorite links to sites related to their profession, industry, or interests. In a corporate or institutional site, a well-edited, well-maintained "Other useful sites" page may be the most valuable and heavily used resource.

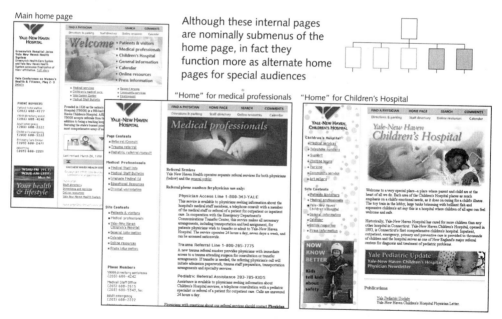

Main home page

Although these internal pages are nominally submenus of the home page, in fact they function more as alternate home pages for special audiences

"Home" for medical professionals   "Home" for Children's Hospital

Unlike print media, where the physical heft and dimensions of a book or magazine give instant cues to the amount of information to expect, Web sites often give few explicit indications of the depth and extent of the content available. This is especially true when the home page does not provide an extensive listing of internal site links. Although search facilities offer users quick access to your content, they are no substitute for a clear, well-organized exposition of your site's contents. Even the best search engines are relatively stupid and have only the most primitive means of assessing the priority, relevance, and interrelations of the information resources you offer in your Web site.

Tables of contents and keyword indexes of the information in your Web site are an easy way to give readers a clear sense of the extent, organization, and context of your site content. Tables of contents and indexes are familiar print conventions; readers understand them and will appreciate the overviews, perspectives, and efficient navigation they afford. The main difference between Web-based indexes and their print counterparts is that a Web site index need not be as extensive or detailed as a book index because you can always use a search engine to find every obscure reference to a keyword. A Web site index should point to the most relevant and useful occurrences of a keyword and ignore minor references (those will turn up in a keyword search anyway).

Site maps give the reader a graphic overview of the site contents. The form of site maps varies from hierarchical branching diagrams to geographic metaphors, but they all share the same limitations:

- Site maps of complex Web sites are at best simple metaphors that convey only the approximate outlines of the site content. Computer screens offer limited space, so site map graphics tend to oversimplify and exaggerate hierarchies of information. The results are seldom worth the time and expense involved, unless you mean to convey only the broadest outlines of the site structure. Unless your Web site deals with information that is inherently spatial (a set of maps, for instance), text-based tables of contents or indexes will always be more efficient and informative.
- Site maps are inherently graphic and are thus harder and more costly to change than text lists when (inevitably) your site is reorganized or you add information.

"WHAT'S NEW?" PAGES

Many Web sites need to be updated frequently so that the information they present doesn't become stale. But the presence of new information may not be obvious to readers unless you make a systematic effort to inform them. If items that appear on your home page menu are updated, you could place a "NEW" graphic next to each updated item. If, however, your site is complex with many levels of information spread over dozens (or hundreds) of pages, you might consider making a "What's New" page designed specifically to inform users of updated information throughout the site.

Every Web page in a corporate or institutional site should carry a revision date that is changed each time the page is updated so that users can be sure they have the latest version. Many readers print pages from the Web. Without a revision date, your readers have no way of telling whether the page they printed is current or outdated.

SEARCH FEATURES

Search facilities are a necessity for large sites and are convenient even for smaller sites that contain long documents. Sites that are updated frequently also require a good search engine, because your menus and site index will probably not keep pace with every change you make in the content pages of the site. But search engines are no substitute for a carefully organized browsing structure of menus and submenus. The two systems, browsing by menu and searching by keyword, complement each other – neither system alone is adequate. Keyword searches give the reader specific links to follow but with no overview of the nature and extent of your content and no feel for how you have organized the information. Menus and tables of contents are great for broad overviews, but if your readers are looking for a specific piece of information not mentioned in the contents, they may miss what you have to offer.

The search software you use will often dictate the user interface for searching. If you update your content frequently, be sure that your search engine's indexing is done at least daily. Also be sure that your readers understand exactly what content is being searched: the entire Web site or just a

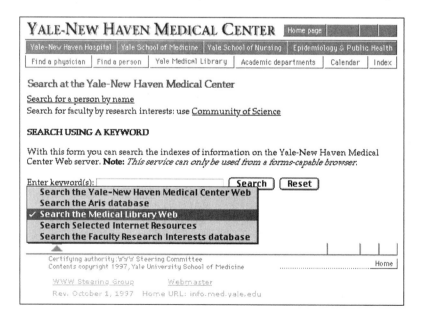

subsection? If your site is complex you may wish to offer readers a pop-up menu that lists the areas of your site and allows them to limit their search to a specific area. And make sure that the results page matches the graphic design of the site.

CONTACT INFORMATION AND USER FEEDBACK

The Web is a bidirectional medium – people expect to be able to send you comments, questions, and suggestions. Always provide at least one link to an email address in a prominent location in your site. You can request user information and feedback using Web page forms and then use a database to store and analyze their input.

The logistical and support staff implications of creating a popular Web site are often overlooked until a crisis develops. Rolling out a new, heavily trafficked Web site is like suddenly adding a second front door to your enterprise. Who will greet the people who come flooding in? Who will answer their questions about your organization and its products and services? Who will collect and analyze the information you receive from your readers? Before you add this functionality to your Web pages, be sure you have an infrastructure in place to handle the fruits of your success.

Street addresses, phone numbers, fax numbers It is amazing how often site developers forget that not all communication with the organization goes through the Web site. Even if you have a great Web site, people will still want to call you, send you mail and express packages, and fax you documents. Your home page should include the same contact information you provide on your stationery, marketing materials, and business cards. If your home page design doesn't allow adequate space for this information, at least provide a link to another page with contact information.

Maps, travel directions, parking information Your Web site is an ideal place to make travel information available to clients, visitors, vendors – anyone who needs to find your organization. Graphic maps, text-based directions, local hotel information, and even internal floor plans can ensure that your visitors will be able to reach you easily and efficiently.

BIBLIOGRAPHIES AND APPENDIXES

The concept of "documents" in electronic environments like the Web is flexible, and the economics and logistics of digital publishing make it possible to provide information without the costs associated with printing paper documents. Making a report available to colleagues on paper usually means printing a copy for each person, so costs and practicality dictate that paper reports be concise and with limited supporting material. Bibliographies, glossaries, or appendixes that might be too bulky to load into a task force report or committee recommendations document can instead be placed in a Web site, making the information available to colleagues as needed.

FAQ PAGES

The Web and other Internet-based media have evolved a unique institution, the FAQ, or "frequently asked questions" page, where the most commonly asked questions from users are listed along with answers. FAQ pages are ideal for Web sites designed to provide support and information to a working group within an institution or to a professional or trade group that maintains a central office staff. Most questions from new users have been asked and answered many times before. A well-designed FAQ page can improve users' understanding of the information and services offered and reduce demands on your support staff.

CUSTOM SERVER ERROR PAGES

Most Web users are familiar with the "404 error, file not found" screens that pop up on the screen when a Web server is unable to locate a page. The file may be missing because the author has moved or deleted it, or the reader may simply have typed or copied the URL of the page incorrectly. One mark of a really polished Web site is custom-designed and *useful* error and server message pages. Most standard error screens are generic, ugly, and uninformative. A well-designed error screen should be consistent with the graphic look and feel of the rest of the Web site. The page should offer some likely explanations for the error, suggest alternatives, and provide links to the local home page, site index, or search page:

INTERNET VERSUS INTRANET DESIGN

Most Web sites are designed to be viewed by audiences inside an organization and are often not visible to the larger World Wide Web. Although these intranet sites employ the same technology as sites designed for the larger Web audience, their design and content should reflect the different motivations of intranet users.

External sites are usually aimed at capturing an audience. The overall goal is to maximize contact time, drawing readers deeper into the site and rewarding their curiosity with interesting or entertaining information. One assumption that governs Web design is that readers may have little motivation to stay and must be constantly enticed and rewarded with rich graphics or compelling information to linger within the site.

Successful intranet sites assemble useful information, organize it into logical systems, and deliver the information efficiently. You don't want intranet users lingering over their Web browsers, either in frustration at not being able to find what they are seeking or in idle "surfing." Allow employees and students to get exactly what they need quickly and then move on.

The evolution of the Web   In most institutions the use of the World Wide Web has evolved over the past few years from an informal collection of personal or group home pages into a semiorganized collection of sites listed in one or more master home pages or "front door" sites. Ironically, universities and companies that adopted the Web early are often the least organized, because each department and group has over the years evolved its own idiosyncratic approach to graphic design, user interface design, and information architecture. But the Web and institutional intranets are no longer just a playground for the local "geeks." Patchy, heterogeneous design standards and a lack of cohesive central planning can cripple any attempt to realize productivity gains through an intranet.

Sun Microsystem's Internet and intranet sites are models of a consistent, in-depth approach to Web design. User surveys show that the average Sun employee uses about twelve intranet pages a day and about two new intranet subsites each week. Sun's user interface expert Jakob Nielsen estimates that his redesign of Sun's intranet user interface may save each employee as much as five minutes a week through consistent companywide application of design and navigation interface standards. The aggregate savings in Sun employee time may amount to as much as ten million dollars a year, through

improving productivity and increasing the efficiency with which employees use the company's intranet sites.

DESIGN STANDARDS

All institutions that deploy intranets have clear economic and social motivations to develop and propagate a consistent set of design standards for the development of local Web pages and internal information sources. But obstacles to implementing an institutionwide set of standards are considerable. Groups and individuals may feel that they own the "right" to design and publish as they please, and they often have more Web expertise and experience than senior management. Groups that have used the Web for years already have a considerable investment in their designs and will be reluctant to change. University and nonprofit administrations often lack the economic resources to develop institutional standards manuals and motivate departments to adopt them. The lack of broad consensus on what constitutes proper Web design only complicates the matter.

User-centered design   The problems cited above will be familiar to every university or corporate Webmaster and to anyone who has had to sit on a Web or intranet committee. They are all great reasons for doing nothing, but they ignore the most important element of any intranet – the user. If reasonable, consistent design standards are not adopted, the average intranet user suffers confusion, reduced productivity, and lost opportunity to benefit from the promise of intranet technologies. The advantages of consistent graphic design and user interface standards are immediately obvious in a user-centered approach to intranet design and clearly transcend the parochial interests of participating departments, groups, and individuals. If the typical user of an intranet sees more confusion than useful information, no one will benefit.

Without clear design standards, your intranet will evolve as a patchy, confusing set of pages – some well-designed, some disastrous, and all mere parts of a dysfunctional system. A lack of design standards also limits intranet use by imposing complex design decisions on new users who would like to develop intranet sites; it's a daunting task to have to develop new graphic design and interface conventions instead of being able to adopt a professionally designed system of corporate intranet standards.

4 *Page Design*

Clutter and confusion are failures of design,
not attributes of information.
– Edward Tufte, 1997 interview

WE SEEK CLARITY, order, and trustworthiness in information sources, whether traditional paper documents or Web pages. Effective page design can provide this confidence. The spatial organization of graphics and text on the Web page can engage readers with graphic impact, direct their attention, prioritize the information they see, and make their interactions with your Web site more enjoyable and efficient.

Visual logic Graphic design creates visual logic and seeks an optimal balance between visual sensation and graphic information. Without the visual impact of shape, color, and contrast, pages are graphically boring and will not motivate the viewer. Dense text documents without contrast and visual relief are also harder to read, particularly on the relatively low-resolution screens of personal computers. But without the depth and complexity of text, highly graphical pages risk disappointing the user by offering a poor balance of visual sensation, text information, and interactive hypermedia links. In seeking this ideal balance, the primary design constraints are the restrictions of HTML and the bandwidth limitations on user access speeds that range from 28.8 KBPS (kilobits per second) modems to Ethernet.

Visual and functional continuity in your Web site organization, graphic design, and typography are essential to convince your audience that your Web site offers them timely, accurate, and useful information. A careful, systematic approach to page design can simplify navigation, reduce user errors, and make it easier for readers to take advantage of the information and features of the site.

VISUAL HIERARCHY

The primary task of graphic design is to create a strong, consistent visual hierarchy in which important elements are emphasized and content is organized logically and predictably.

Graphic design is visual information management, using the tools of layout, typography, and illustration to lead the reader's eye through the page. Readers first see pages as large masses of shape and color, with foreground elements contrasted against the background field. Only secondarily do they begin to pick out specific information, first from graphics if they are present, and only then do they start parsing the harder medium of text and begin to read individual words and phrases:

Visual scanning of page structure over time

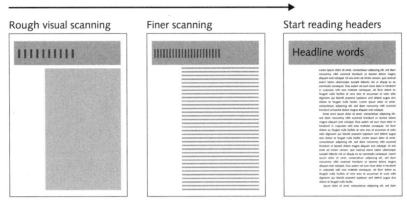

Rough visual scanning Finer scanning Start reading headers

Contrast is essential   The overall graphic balance and organization of the page is crucial to drawing the reader into your content. A dull page of solid text will repel the eye as a mass of undifferentiated gray, without obvious cues to the structure of your information. A page dominated by poorly designed or overly bold graphics or typography also will distract or repel users looking for substantive content. You will need to strike an appropriate balance between attracting the eye with visual contrast and providing a sense of organization:

Dull; no focal points,
no graphic structure

Stronger visual structure;
better contrast

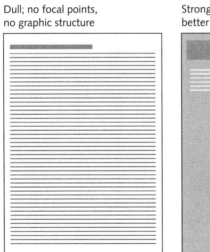

Visual balance and appropriateness to the intended audience are the keys to successful design decisions. The most effective designs for general (mostly modem-based) Internet audiences use a careful balance of text and links with relatively small graphics. These pages load into viewers quickly, even when accessed from 28.8 modems, yet still achieve substantial graphic impact:

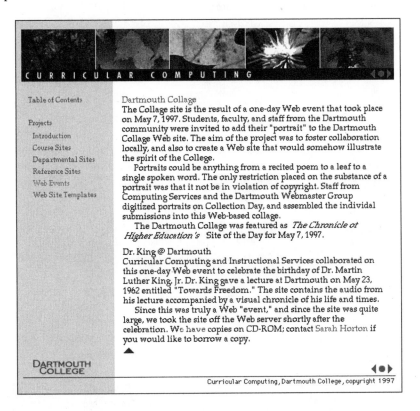

When establishing a page design for your Web site, consider your overall purpose, the nature of your content, and, most important, the expectations of your readers.

CONSISTENCY

Establish a layout grid and a style for handling your text and graphics, then apply it consistently to build rhythm and unity across the pages of your site. Repetition is not boring; it gives your site a consistent graphic identity that creates and then reinforces a distinct sense of "place" and makes your site distinct and memorable. A consistent approach to layout and navigation allows readers to adapt quickly to your design and predict with confidence the location of information and navigation controls across the pages of your site.

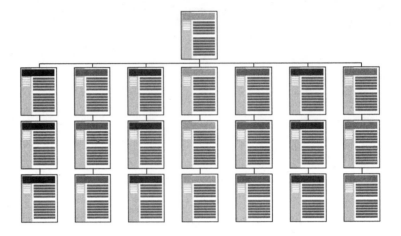

If you choose a graphic theme, use it throughout your Web site. Meta-Design's home page banner, below, sets the graphic theme for the site and introduces distinctive typography and a set of navigation icons:

Below is a banner at the top of an interior page in MetaDesign's site. Note how the typography and the icon theme are carried through to the interior banners. There is no confusion about whose site you are navigating through:

PAGE DIMENSIONS

Although Web pages and conventional print documents share many graphic, functional, and editorial similarities, the computer screen, not a printed page, is the primary delivery site for Web-based information, and the computer screen is very different from the printed page. Computer screens are typically smaller than most opened books or magazines. A common mistake in Web design is spreading the width of page graphics beyond the area most viewers can see on their fourteen- or fifteen-inch display screens:

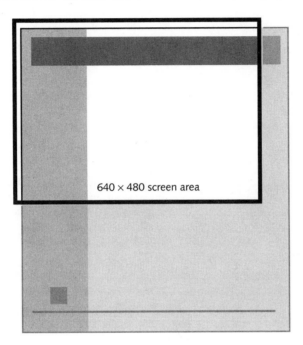

640 × 480 screen area

GRAPHIC SAFE AREAS

The "safe area" for Web page graphics is determined by two factors: the minimum screen size in common use today (640 × 480 pixels) and the width of paper used to print Web pages.

Most monitors used in academia and business are fourteen to fifteen inches (thirty-five to thirty-eight centimeters) in size, and they are usually set to display a 640 × 480-pixel screen. Web page graphics that exceed the width dimension of these small monitors look amateurish and will inconvenience many readers by forcing them to scroll both horizontally and vertically to see the full page layout. It's bad enough to have to scroll in one (vertical) direction; having to scroll in two directions is intolerable.

Even on small monitors it is possible to display graphics that are too wide to print well on common letter-size, legal-size, or A4 paper widths. However, in many Web pages printing is a secondary concern. Just be aware that your readers will lose the right three-quarters of an inch (two centimeters) of your layout if they print wide pages in standard vertical print layout. Pages with lots of text should *always* be designed to print properly, because most readers will print those pages to read them more comfortably, and if the layout page is too wide readers will lose several words from each line of text down the right margin .

The graphic safe area dimensions for printing layouts and for page layouts designed to use the maximum width of a 640 × 480-pixel screen are shown below.

Graphic "safe area" dimensions for layouts designed to print well:
   Maximum width = 535 pixels
   Maximum height = 295 pixels

Graphic "safe area" dimensions for layouts designed to maximize screen usage:
   Maximum width = 595 pixels
   Maximum height = 295 pixels

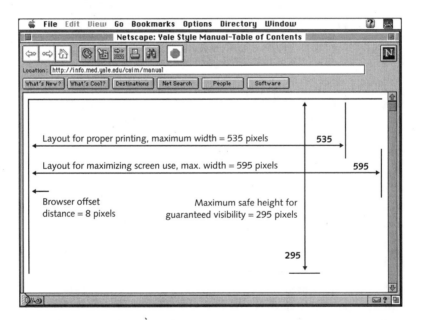

Graphic safe areas, 640 × 480 screens
Dimensions account for both Netscape Navigator and Internet Explorer, in both Windows95/NT and Macintosh versions. Note that if you choose to maximize the width of your page layout, you may lose about two centimeters off the right edge of the page when it is printed.

PAGE LENGTH

Determining the proper length for any Web page requires balancing four factors:

1 The relation between page and screen size
2 The content of your documents
3 Whether the reader is expected to browse the content online or to print or download the documents for later reading
4 The bandwidth available to your audience

Researchers have noted the disorientation that results from scrolling on computer screens. The reader's loss of context is particularly troublesome when such basic navigational elements as document titles, site identifiers, and links to other site pages disappear off-screen. This effect argues for the creation of navigational Web pages (especially home pages and menus) that contain no more than one or two 640 × 480 screens' worth of information and that feature local navigational links at the beginning and end of the page layout. Long Web pages require the user to remember too much information that scrolls off the screen; users easily lose their sense of context when the navigational buttons or major links are not visible:

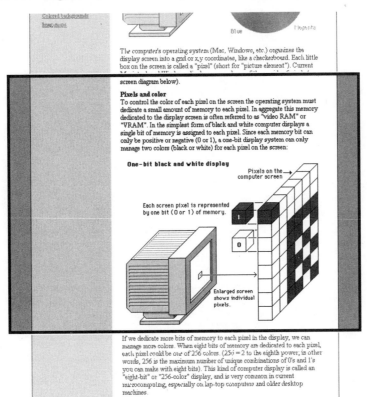

Scrolling In long Web pages the user must depend on the vertical scroll bar slider (the little box within the scroll bar) to navigate. In some graphic interfaces (Macintosh, Windows 3.1) the scroll bar slider is fixed in size and provides little indication of the document length relative to what's visible on the screen, so the reader gets no visual cue to page length. In very long Web pages small movements of the scroll bar can completely change the visual contents of the screen, leaving the reader no familiar landmarks to orient by. This gives the user no choice but to crawl downward with the scroll bar arrows or risk missing sections of the page.

Long Web pages do have their advantages, however. They are often easier for managers to organize and for users to download. Web site managers don't have to maintain as many links and pages with longer documents, and users don't need to download multiple files to collect information on a topic. Long pages are particularly useful for providing information that you don't expect users to read online (realistically, that means any document longer than two printed pages). You can make long pages friendlier by positioning "jump to top buttons" at intervals equivalent to one small screenful of page (about 295 vertical pixels). That way the user will never have to scroll more than about half a screen to find a navigation button that quickly brings him or her back to the top of the page.

All Web pages longer than two vertical screens should have a jump button at the foot of the page:

Jump to top of page

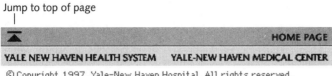

If a Web page is too long, however, or contains too many large graphics, the page can take too long for users with slow connections to download. Very large Web pages with many graphics may also overwhelm the RAM (random access memory) limitations of the user's Web browser, causing the browser to crash or causing the page to display and print improperly.

CONTENT AND PAGE LENGTH

It makes sense to keep closely related information within the confines of a single Web page, particularly when you expect the user to print or save the text. Keeping the content in one place makes printing or saving easier. But more than four screens' worth of information forces the user to scroll so much that the utility of the online version of the page begin to deteriorate. Long pages often fail to take advantage of the linkages available in the Web medium.

If you wish to provide both a good online interface for a long page and easy printing or saving of its content:

- Divide the page into chunks of no more than one to two printed pages' worth of information, including inlined graphics or figures. Use the power of hypertext links to take advantage of the Web medium.
- Provide a link to a separate file that contains the full-length text combined as one page, designed so the reader can print or save all the related information in one step. Don't forget to include the URL of the online version within the text of that page so that users can find updates and correctly cite the source.

In general, you should favor shorter Web pages for:
- Home pages and menu or navigation pages elsewhere in your site
- Documents to be browsed and read online
- Pages with very large graphics

In general, longer documents are:
- Easier to maintain (content is in one piece, not in linked chunks)
- More like the structure of their paper counterparts (not chopped up)
- Easier for users to download and print

DESIGN GRIDS FOR WEB PAGES

Consistency and predictability are essential attributes of any well-designed information system. The design grids that underlie most well-designed paper publications are equally necessary in designing electronic documents and online publications, where the spatial relations among on-screen elements are constantly shifting in response to the user's input and system activity.

Grids bring order to the page Current implementations of HyperText Markup Language do not allow the easy flexibility or control that graphic designers routinely expect from page layout software or multimedia authoring tools. Yet HTML can be used to create complex and highly functional information systems if it is used thoughtfully. When used inappropriately or inconsistently, the typographic controls and inlined graphics of Web pages can create a confusing visual jumble, without apparent hierarchy of importance. Haphazardly mixed graphics and text decrease usability and legibility, just as they do in paper pages. A balanced and consistently implemented design scheme will increase readers' confidence in your site.

Poor page layout, no visual hierarchy   Better layout, balanced

No one design grid system is appropriate for all Web pages. Your first step is to establish a basic layout grid. With this graphic "backbone" you can determine how the major blocks of type and illustrations will regularly occur in your pages and set the placement and style guidelines for major screen titles, subtitles, and navigation links or buttons. To start, gather representative examples of your text, along with some graphics, scans, or other illustrative material, and experiment with various arrangements of the elements on the page. In larger projects it isn't possible to predict how every combination of text and graphics will interact on the screen, but examine your Web layout "sketches" against both your most complex and your least complex pages.

Your goal is to establish a consistent, logical screen layout, one that allows you to "plug in" text and graphics without having to stop and rethink your basic design approach on each new page. Without a firm underlying design grid, your project's page layout will be driven by the problems of the moment, and the overall design of your Web site will seem patchy and confusing.

Vertical stratification in Web pages A Web page can be almost any length, but you've only got about thirty square inches "above the fold" – at the top of your page – to capture the average reader, because that is all he or she will see as the page loads. One crucial difference between Web page design and print page design is that when readers turn a book or magazine page they see not only the whole next page but the whole two-page spread, all at the same time. In print design, therefore, the two-page spread is the fundamental graphic design unit.

Print design can achieve a design unity and density of information that Web page design cannot emulate. Regardless of how large the display monitor is, the reader still sees one page at a time, and even a twenty-one-inch monitor will display only as much information as is found in a typical magazine spread:

Book pages

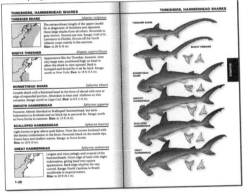

Book spreads are seen as units of two pages;
Web pages are always single units, regardless of
monitor size

Web page on a seventeen-inch monitor (1024 × 768 pixels)

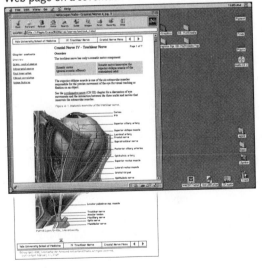

Design for screens of information   Most Web page designs can be divided vertically into zones with different functions and varying levels of graphics and text complexity. As the page is progressively revealed by vertical scrolling, new content appears and the upper content disappears. A new graphic context is established each time the reader scrolls down the page. Web page layouts should thus be judged not by viewing the whole page as a unit but by dividing the page into visual and functional zones and judging the suitability of each screen of information. Notice the vertical structure of Yale–New Haven Hospital's home page. The top screen of information is much denser with links because it is the only area sure to be visible to all users:

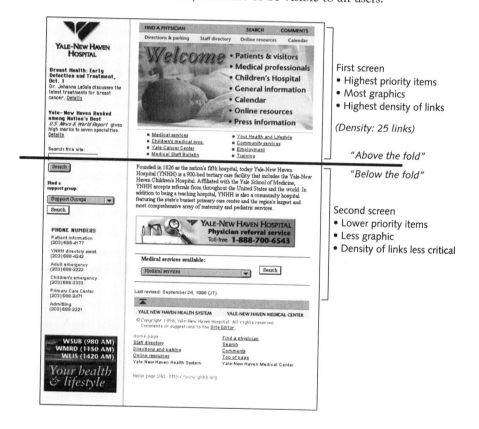

Sample page grid   When we designed our online Web style manual (info. med.yale.edu/caim/manual) we used a basic Web page grid that incorporates an image map with paging buttons at the top and bottom of each page. A "scan column" along the left side of the page does two jobs: it provides space for local links to related material, and it gives visual relief by narrowing the right text column to about sixty to seventy characters per line. The diagram on the facing page shows the major repeating components of the style manual pages:

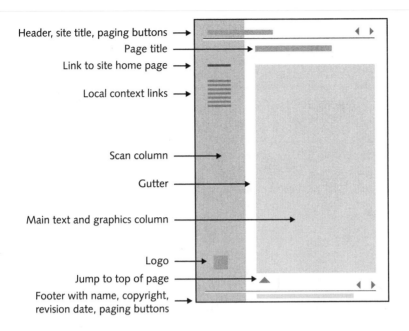

Header, site title, paging buttons →
Page title →
Link to site home page →
Local context links →
Scan column →
Gutter →
Main text and graphics column →
Logo →
Jump to top of page →
Footer with name, copyright, revision date, paging buttons →

Here we show the "invisible" table (BORDER="0") that underlies the column structure of the page, with the critical page dimensions:

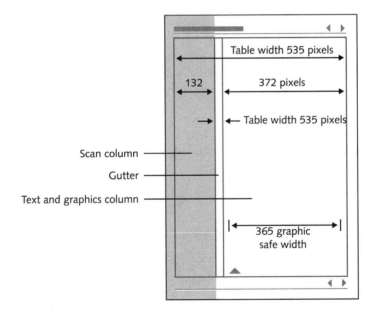

Table width 535 pixels

132

372 pixels

← Table width 535 pixels

Scan column
Gutter
Text and graphics column

365 graphic safe width

We chose 535 pixels as the maximum dimension for the page layout because that is the widest table that will print on a standard letter-size page. With a few exceptions, all graphics for the online manual were designed to fit within the 365-pixel "safe area" of the text column.

PAGE HEADERS AND FOOTERS

Many Web authors surrender to the giddy thrills of large home page graphics, forgetting that a Web page is not just a visual experience – it has to function efficiently to retain its appeal to the user. Remember that the page builds its graphic impact only gradually as it is downloaded to the user. The best measure of the efficiency of a page design is the number of options available for readers within the top four inches of the page. A big, bold graphic may tease casual Web surfers, but if it takes the average reader a full minute to download the top of your page, and there are few links to be seen until he or she scrolls down the page (causing even longer delays), then you may lose a big part of your audience before you offer them links to the rest of your site.

PAGE HEADERS: SITE IDENTITY

Careful graphic design will give your Web site a unique visual identity. A "signature" graphic and page layout allows the reader to grasp immediately the purpose of the document and its relation to other pages. Graphics used within headers can also signal the relatedness of a series of Web pages. Unlike designers of print documents, designers of Web systems can never be sure what other pages the reader has seen before linking to the current page. Yale–New Haven Hospital's many Web pages and subsites all include a signature header graphic that is also an imagemap with basic navigation links included:

FIND A PHYSICIAN	HOME PAGE	SEARCH	COMMENTS
Directions & parking	Staff directory	Online resources	Calendar

Even if you choose not to use graphics on your pages, the header area of every Web page should contain a prominent title at or near its top. Graphics placed above the title line should not be so large that they force the title and introductory text off the page on standard office-size monitors. In a related series of documents there may also be subtitles, section titles, or other text elements that convey the relation of the displayed document to others in the series. To be effective, these title elements must be standardized across all the pages in your site.

PAGE FOOTERS: PROVENANCE

Every Web page should contain basic data about the origin and age of the page, but this repetitive and prosaic information does not need to be placed at the top of the page. Remember, too, that by the time readers have scrolled to the bottom of your Web page the navigation links you might have provided at the top may no longer be visible. Well-designed page footers offer the user a set of links to other pages in addition to essential data about the site.

The pages in Yale–New Haven Hospital's Web site all carry a distinctive footer graphic with a consistent visual and functional identity:

PAGE LAYOUT

Laying out Web pages involves a bit of wizardry. HTML was designed by engineers and scientists who never envisioned it as a page layout tool. Their aim was to provide a way to describe structural information about a document, not a tool to determine a document's appearance. Once the real world started to work on the Web, graphic designers began adapting the primitive tools of HTML to produce documents that looked more like their print counterparts. The point was not to produce "jazzier" or "prettier" pages. The layout conventions of print documents have evolved over hundreds of years for concrete and practical reasons, and they offer many functional advantages over the plain, single-column page layout envisioned by the original designers of the World Wide Web.

Introduction to ISO

What are standards ?

Standards are documented agreements containing technical specifications or other precise criteria to be used consistently as rules, guidelines, or definitions of characteristics, to ensure that materials, products, processes and services are fit for their purpose.

For example, the format of the credit cards, phone cards, and "smart" cards that have become commonplace is derived from an ISO International Standard. Adhering to the standard, which defines such features as an optimal thickness (0,76 mm), means that the cards can be used worldwide.

International Standards thus contribute to making life simpler, and to increasing the reliability and effectiveness of the goods and services we use.

What is ISO ?

The International Organization for Standardization (ISO) is a worldwide federation of national standards bodies from some 100 countries, one from each country.

ISO is a non-governmental organization established in 1947. The mission of ISO is to promote the development of standardization and related activities in the world with a view to facilitating the international exchange of goods and services, and to developing cooperation in the spheres of intellectual, scientific, technological and economic activity.

ISO's work results in international agreements which are published as International Standards.

If you simply place a chunk of text on a Web page, the line length will be determined by the dimensions of the viewer's browser window. When the user resizes his or her window, the text reflows to fill the new space. Although some people may consider this a "feature," it hinders the user's experience with the content. All the issues of legibility, readability, and style that we discuss in this manual rely on the Web designer's ability to position words, images, and screen elements on the "page" in a way that adheres to established typographic conventions. Without some adherence to these standards you may confuse and ultimately lose your readers.

Because of the limitations of HTML, the only layout tool for site designers at this time is tables.

Line length One of the main typographical failings of the standard Web interface is the lack of adherence to standard line lengths. Reading becomes uncomfortable when there are more than about twelve words per line. If there is a long distance between the end of a line and the beginning of the next line, the eye has to make a significant shift to return to the left margin. Also, if the eye must traverse great distances on a page, the reader is easily lost and must hunt for the beginning of the next line. Quantitative studies show that moderate line lengths significantly increase the legibility of text. Use tables to limit the line length, ideally to ten to twelve words per line.

Margins Margins define the reading area of your page by separating the main text from nontext elements, such as interface elements and other unrelated graphics. Margins also provide contrast and visual interest. Use table cells to establish margins, and use them consistently throughout your site to provide unity.

Columns　One common use of tables that increases both legibility and functionality of page layouts is a dual scan column–text column layout. A narrow vertical scan column along the left side of the page does two useful things: it provides flexible space for variations in page layout, and it narrows the text column to a comfortable line length.

Gutters　In print the space between columns is called a gutter. Gutters keep columns from running into one another:

Columns without gutter

You can use tables to create gutters in three ways: (1) by adding a cell to your table that functions as the gutter, (2) by using the CELLPADDING attribute of the TABLE tag (the space between the cell contents and the cell), and (3) by using the CELLSPACING attribute of the TABLE tag (the space surrounding the cell):

Table with cell gutter　　　　Table with CELLPADDING　　　　Table with CELLSPACING

Borders   When we talk about tables we are not speaking of the beveled beauties that HTML offers to present tabular content. We are using tables to get around the limitations of HTML, and we are using them in ways for which they were not intended. These are invisible tables whose sole purpose is to give us control over page elements, so be sure to set BORDER="0" in your TABLE tag. And if you do use tables to present tabular information, use spacing, alignment, and indents, not borders, to delimit tabular information.

ChemLab | Info | Techniques | Chem 3/5 | Chem 6

The Chemistry 3/5 Laboratory

Week 6: Acids, bases, and buffers, cont.

Introduction & goals
Chemistry & background
Key questions
Prelab problems
Safety
Procedures
In your write-up

Back to Experiments
ChemLab Home

Possible Unknown Acids, Bases, and Buffers

This Table contains the possible acids and conjugate acids of possible bases. Buffers could be composed of any tabulated acid and its conjugate base.

Table 1: Weak Acids, Ka, and pKa values

Acid	HA	A^-	K_a	pKa
Acetic	CH_3COOH	CH_3COO^-	1.76×10^{-5}	4.75
Ammonium Ion	NH_4^+	NH_3	5.6×10^{-10}	9.25
Benzoic	C_6H_5COOH	$C_6H_5COO^-$	6.46×10^{-5}	4.19
Carbonic	H_2CO_3	HCO_3^-	4.3×10^{-7}	6.37
	HCO_3^-	CO_3^{2-}	4.8×10^{-11}	10.32
Chloroacetic	$CH_2ClCOOH$	CH_2ClCOO^-	1.4×10^{-3}	2.85
Formic	$HCOOH$	$HCOO^-$	1.77×10^{-4}	3.75
Oxalic	$H_2C_2O_4$	$HC_2O_4^-$	5.9×10^{-2}	1.23
	$HC_2O_4^-$	$C_2O_4^{2-}$	6.4×10^{-5}	4.19
Phosphoric	H_3PO_4	$H_2PO_4^-$	7.52×10^{-3}	2.12
	$H_2PO_4^-$	HPO_4^{-2}	6.23×10^{-8}	7.21
	HPO_4^{2-}	PO_4^{3-}	2.2×10^{-13}	12.67

ChemLab

CELL ATTRIBUTES AND TABLE DIMENSIONS

The behavior of an HTML table depends largely on how its cells are defined. One "feature" of tables is that they try to be accommodating; they expand and collapse to fit the dimensions of the viewer's browser window. In their most basic form, tables are not much more precise than plain text.

To make tables a useful tool for page layout, first you must define cell widths with absolute values. This will keep the tables from expanding to fill the window. Then, to keep tables from collapsing when the browser window is too small to accommodate their dimensions, include an invisible image equal to the width of the cell in each table cell. These two techniques will force table cells to maintain their dimensions regardless of the size of the browser window. To summarize:

- Use fixed-width table cells
- Include invisible images to maintain table dimensions

Italics — Italicized text attracts the eye because it contrasts in shape from body text. Use italics for convention — book or periodical titles, for example — or within text for stressed or foreign words or phrases. However, do not set large blocks of text in italics since the readability of italicized text, particularly at screen resolutions, is much less than with roman faces.

Bold — Boldface text gives emphasis because it contrasts in color from the body text. Section subheads work well set in bold. Boldface text is readable on screen, though large blocks of text set in bold lack contrast and therefore lose their effectiveness.

Underlining — Underlined text is a carryover from the days of the typewriter, where options like italics or boldface were not available.

Variable-width tables reflow to fill the browser window

Fixed-width tables maintain their dimensions regardless of the size of the browser window

ADVANCED TABLES

ALIGNMENT

Tables can be used to combine different text alignment specifications. In this example the text in the left column is right justified, and the text in the right is left justified.

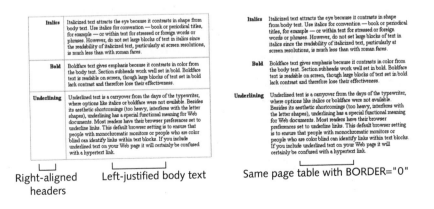

Right-aligned headers | Left-justified body text

Same page table with BORDER="0"

Tables give the designer much greater flexibility in positioning images on a page than simple inline image placement. You can use tables to create complex layouts that combine text and images or multimedia materials. The example below is depicted with borders both on and off to show the underlying table used to establish the layout:

Standard two-column page table

Embedded table for indented menu

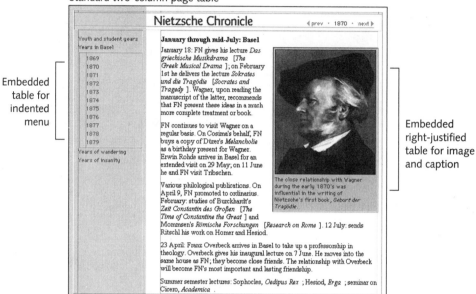

Embedded right-justified table for image and caption

Same page table with BORDER="0"

Something fancy you can do with tables is to take a composite image, split it in pieces, and then recombine it in the cells of a table. This technique is useful for creating wraparound effects or image captions. The following example is depicted with borders on and off to show how the table is formatted:

HTML text caption   Composite image split into
two pieces and recombined
in a page table

Same page table with BORDER="0"

Watch out for hard returns in your HTML code when using tables to join an image. A hard return before a closing table data tag (</TD>) will add space between the table cells. You will also need to set the CELLPADDING, CELLSPACING, and BORDER parameters of the TABLE tag to zero in order for the image to join correctly. Finally, be sure to include an invisible image to keep the cells in your tables from collapsing (see *Cell attributes and table dimensions,* above).

FRAMES

Frames are *meta*-documents that call and display multiple HTML documents in a single browser window. A frame document contains no body HTML tags, just the parameters for the frames and the URLs of the HTML documents designated to fill them. Frames-based pages do not function as an integrated unit, which is both good and bad. Frames are useful for certain content and greatly facilitate site maintenance. They provide a good way to maintain narrative and design consistency in your site; you can split the browser screen between site navigation and the material you wish to bring up with a link. But frames also impose interface and design limitations. Frames can easily confuse readers who wish to print material on a page or bookmark a page for later reference or navigate using the browser's "Forward" and "Back" buttons. And screen space becomes an issue with frames; if you use frames to divide the browser screen, you will force many readers to scroll to see the full contents of each frame.

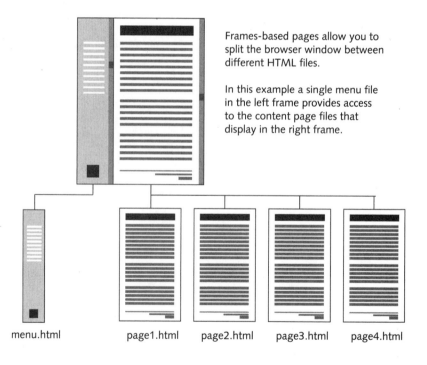

Frames-based pages allow you to split the browser window between different HTML files.

In this example a single menu file in the left frame provides access to the content page files that display in the right frame.

menu.html   page1.html   page2.html   page3.html   page4.html

FLEXIBILITY

Frames are useful in a site whose contents are expected to change frequently. Because a frames-based site can be designed to have a single file for navigation, if you add or remove pages from the site you will have to modify only that one file. Our online Web style guide, for example, requires that a number of files be changed if we add or delete a page because each page in the site has its own navigation column. If we had used frames in our design, we would have had a single file for the section menu, and when we needed to add a page, only that file would have had to be changed to reflect the addition. As it is, when we add a page to a section we must edit each file in that section to add the new link to the navigation column.

FUNCTIONALITY

Frames can give a targeted area of your site a functional coherence. Say your site contains a collection of poems by Emily Dickinson. You could create a virtual "reading room" for her poetry using frames, with the leftmost frame providing the navigation links and the main frame at the right displaying the poems. Because most visitors linger in this area and would use the links you provide for navigation, the quirky navigation of the "Back" button would not be too intrusive.

You can also use frames to provide additional interactivity to your page. Frames allow you to put a page up on the user's screen and change its contents without rewriting the screen. The frames can interact; clicking a link in one frame can change the contents of the other. For example, a text with annotations in one frame can be linked to a footer frame, so that clicking on the text reference fills the footer frame with the corresponding note:

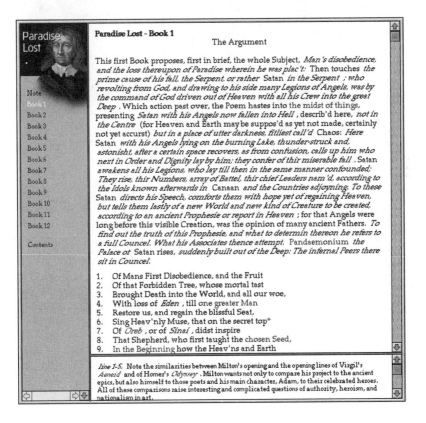

You can use frames to give users more choice in accessing content. This is particularly significant when you are working with large files. Say, for example, you have a movie file that you would like to place on your page with other elements such as text, but you want the download to be optional. If you simply include the HTML tag for the movie on the page with other page elements, the movie will download automatically. With frames, however, you can designate an area of the page as the movie space and give the user a link to click if they wish to download the movie into that space.

AESTHETICS

Many page designers have avoided frames because of their prescribed borders and limited flexibility. Current versions of browser software, however, allow many more frame parameters to be defined. In fact, frame borders can now be set to zero. This allows you to design using the functionality of frames without requiring them to be visual and perhaps inharmonious elements on your page.

GENERAL DESIGN CONSIDERATIONS

Understand the medium   Readers experience Web pages in two ways: as a direct medium where pages are read online and as a delivery medium to access information that is downloaded into text files or printed onto paper. Your expectations about how readers will typically use your site should govern your page design decisions. Documents to be read online should be concise, with the amount of graphics carefully "tuned" to the bandwidth available to your mainstream audience. Documents that will most likely be printed and read offline should appear on one page, and the page width should be narrow enough to print easily on standard paper sizes.

Include fixed page elements   Each page should contain a title, an author, an institutional affiliation, a revision date, copyright information, and a link to the "home page" of your site. Web pages are often printed or saved to disk, and without this information there is no easy way to determine where the document originated. Think of each page in your site as a newspaper clipping, and make sure that the information required to determine its provenance is included.

Don't impose style   Don't set out to develop a "style" for your site, and be careful about simply importing the graphic elements of another Web site or print publication to "decorate" your pages. The graphic and editorial style of your Web site should evolve as a natural consequence of consistent and appropriate handling of your content and page layout.

Maximize prime real estate   In page layout the top of the page is always the most dominant location, but on Web pages the upper page is especially important, because the top four inches of the page are all that is visible on the typical monitor. Use this space efficiently and effectively.

Use subtle colors   Subtle pastel shades of colors typically found in nature make the best choices for background or minor elements. Avoid bold, highly saturated primary colors except in regions of maximum emphasis, and even there use them cautiously.

Beware of graphic embellishments   Horizontal rules, graphic bullets, icons, and other visual markers have their occasional uses, but apply each sparingly (if at all) to avoid a patchy and confusing layout. The same consideration applies to the larger sizes of type on Web pages. One reason professional graphic designers are so impatient with HTML is that the H1 and H2 header tags display in grotesquely large type on most Web browsers. The tools of graphic emphasis are powerful and should be used only in small doses for maximum effect. Overuse of graphic emphasis leads to a "clown's pants" effect in which everything is garish and nothing is emphasized.

CROSS-PLATFORM ISSUES

BROWSER VARIATIONS

Every Web browser interprets HTML tags a little differently. Tables, forms, and graphic positioning and alignment tags will all work a bit differently in each brand or version of Web browser. These subtleties normally pass unnoticed, but in very precise or complex Web page layouts they can lead to nasty surprises. At this writing the two dominant Web browsers are Netscape Navigator 4.0 and Microsoft Internet Explorer 4.0. Both support HTML 3.0, the original 1995 "Netscape extensions" to HTML, plus Javascript and Java, and both share a (mostly) compatible plug-in architecture. But never trust the implementation of any of these advanced features until you have seen your Web pages displayed and working reliably in each brand of browser.

GRAPHICS OFFSET VARIATIONS

Beware of trying to get a graphic that is embedded on your page to line up precisely with a page background image. Offset variations make it a losing cause. The offset is the built-in margin that Web browsers automatically create between the edge of the browser window and the graphics you place on your page:

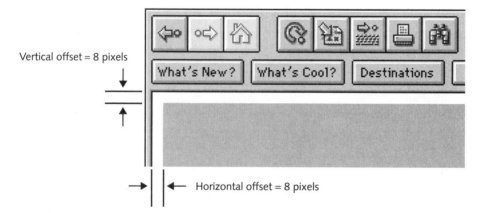

Vertical offset = 8 pixels

Horizontal offset = 8 pixels

If the browser offset was fixed and consistent across browser brands and various hardware platforms, the problem would be manageable, but unfortunately every browser seems to set the vertical and horizontal offsets at slightly different dimensions. Thus even if you have perfectly lined up your foreground and background images in your particular Web browser, you cannot expect the images to line up on someone else's screen. Even within one company the offset may be inconsistent; the various platform versions of Netscape all give slightly different offsets. There are a number of workarounds for this problem; see Siegel 1997 or Weinman 1996 for detailed discussions of this topic.

5 Typography

The satisfaction of the craft comes from elucidating, and perhaps
even ennobling, the text, not from deluding the unwary reader by
applying scents, paints and iron stays to empty prose.
– Robert Bringhurst, *The Elements of Typographic Style*

TYPOGRAPHY is the balance and interplay of letterforms on the page, a verbal and visual equation that helps the reader understand the form and absorb the substance of the page content. Typography plays a dual role as both verbal and visual communication. As readers scan a page they are subconsciously aware of both functions: first they survey the overall graphic patterns of the page, then they parse the language, or read. Good typography establishes a visual hierarchy for rendering prose on the page by providing visual punctuation and graphic accents that help readers understand relations between prose and pictures, headlines and subordinate blocks of text.

CHARACTERISTICS OF TYPE ON THE WEB

Although the basic rules of typography are much the same for both Web pages and conventional print documents, type on-screen and type printed on paper are different in crucial ways. The computer screen renders typefaces at a much lower resolution than is found in books, magazines, and even pages output from inexpensive printers. Most magazine and book typography is rendered at 1200 dots per inch (dpi) or greater, whereas computer screens rarely show more than about 85 dpi. Also, the useable area of typical computer screens is smaller than most magazine and book pages, limiting the information you can deliver on a Web page without scrolling.

But perhaps the most distinctive characteristic of Web typography is its variability. Web pages are built on the fly each time they are loaded into a Web browser. Each line of text, each headline, each unique font and type style is re-created by a complex interaction of the Web browser, the Web server, and the operating system of the reader's computer. The process is fraught with possibilities for the unexpected: a missing font, an out-of-date browser, or a peculiar set of font preferences designated by the reader. You should regard your Web page layouts and typography as *suggestions* of how your pages should be rendered – you'll never know exactly how they will look on the reader's screen.

Page rendered in Palatino

Page rendered in Verdana

CONTENT STRUCTURE AND VISUAL LOGIC

The originators of HTML were scientists who wanted a standard means to share particle physics documents. They had little interest in the exact visual form of the document as seen on the computer screen. In fact, HTML was designed to enforce a clean separation of content structure and graphic design. The intent was to create a World Wide Web of pages that will display in every system and browser available, including browsers that "read" Web page text to visually impaired users and can be accurately interpreted by automated search and analysis engines.

In casting aside the graphic design and editorial management traditions of publishing, the original designers of the Web ignored human motivation. They were so concerned about making Web documents machine-friendly that they produced documents that only machines (or particle physicists) would want to read. In focusing solely on the structural logic of documents they ignored the need for the visual logic of sophisticated graphic design and typography.

For example, most graphic designers avoid using the standard heading tags in HTML (H1, H2, etc.) because they lack subtlety: in most Web browsers these tags make headlines look absurdly large (H1, H2) or ridiculously small (H4, H5, H6). But the header tags in HTML were not created with graphic design in mind. Their sole purpose to designate a hierarchy of headline importance, so that both human readers and automated search engines can look at a document and easily determine its information structure. Only incidentally did browser designers create a visual hierarchy for HTML headers by assigning different type sizes and levels of boldness to each header element.

CASCADING STYLE SHEETS

This division between structural logic and visual logic will eventually be reconciled through the adoption of HTML Cascading Style Sheets (CSS). Style sheets provide control over the exact visual style of headers, paragraphs, lists, and other page elements. For example, if you prefer H3 headers to be set in 12-point Arial bold type, you can specify those details in a style sheet. In this way you can retain the logical use of HTML's structural tags without sacrificing graphic design flexibility. At this writing, however, the major Web browser makers are just beginning to implement CSS support. Although Microsoft Internet Explorer versions 3.0 and 4.0, and Netscape Navigator version 4.0 both support CSS, their exact implementations of it differ. Before you commit to using CSS in your Web design projects, survey your target audience to determine if most of your readers are using a CSS-capable browser.

WHAT WE DO NOW

So what do you do when you know the advantages of preserving the document structure but you want to design Web pages that are attractive enough and functional enough to capture and sustain an audience? You compromise. In the sites we create we use a grab bag of tricks to present as polished and sophisticated a page design as we can manage within the boundaries of "official" HTML (currently HTML 4.0). We use no proprietary HTML tags, such as those specific to Internet Explorer or Netscape Navigator. Our approach to typography emphasizes visual design over structural purity. We believe this is the best compromise until everyone can shift over to a mature implementation of CSS and leave plain HTML behind.

LEGIBILITY

Good typography depends on the visual contrast between one font and another and between text blocks, headlines, and the surrounding white space. Nothing attracts the eye and brain of the reader like strong contrast and distinctive patterns, and you can achieve those attributes only by carefully designing them into your pages. If you cram every page with dense text, readers see a wall of gray and will instinctively reject the lack of visual contrast. Just making things uniformly bigger doesn't help. Even boldface fonts quickly become monotonous, because if everything is bold then nothing stands out "boldly."

When your content is primarily text, typography is the tool you use to "paint" patterns of organization on the page. The first thing the reader sees is not the title or other details on the page but the overall pattern and contrast of the page. The regular, repeating patterns established through carefully organized pages of text and graphics help the reader to establish the location and organization of your information and increase legibility. Patchy, heterogeneous typography and text headers make it hard for the user to see repeating patterns and it almost impossible to predict where information is likely to be in located in unfamiliar documents:

Too patchy, inconsistent

Better layout of type blocks

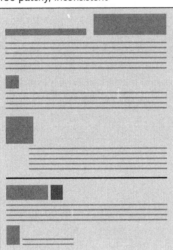
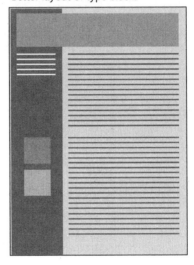

ALIGNMENT

Margins define the reading area of your page by separating the main text from the surrounding environment. Margins provide important visual relief in any document, but careful design of margins and other "white space" is particularly important in Web page design because Web content must coexist on the computer screen with the interface elements of the browser itself and with other windows, menus, and icons of the user interface.

Margins and space can be used to delineate the main text from the other page elements. And when used consistently, margins provide unity throughout a site by creating a consistent structure and look to the site pages. They also add visual interest by contrasting the positive space of the screen (text, graphics) from the negative (white) space.

Web content must share the screen with user interface elements

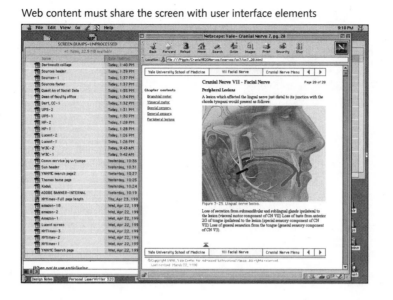

Text blocks have different ways of sitting within margins. Left-justified, centered, right-justified, and, most recently, justified text are the alignment options available on the Web.

Justified text   Justified text is set flush with the left and right margins. Justified blocks of text create solid rectangles, and block headings are normally centered for a symmetrical, formal-looking document. In print, justification is achieved by adjusting the space between words and by using word hyphenation. Page layout programs use a hyphenation dictionary to check for and apply hyphenation at each line's end and then adjust word spacing throughout the line. But even with sophisticated page layout software, justified text blocks often suffer from poor spacing and excessive hyphenation and require manual refinement. This level of control is not even a remote possibility on Web pages. The most recent browser versions (and css) support justified text, but it is achieved by crude adjustments to word spacing. Fine adjustments are not possible on low-resolution computer displays and are impractical to implement in today's Web browsers. Also, Web browsers are unlikely to offer automatic hyphenation any time soon, another "must" for properly justified text. For the foreseeable future, the legibility of your Web documents will suffer if you set your text in justified format.

Centered and right-justified text blocks   Centered and right-justified text blocks are difficult to read. We read from left to right, anchoring our tracking across the page at the vertical line of the left margin. The ragged left margins produced by centering or right-justifying text make that scanning much harder, because your eye needs to search for the beginning of each new line.

Left-justified text   Left-justified text is the most legible option for Web pages because the left margin is even and predictable and the right margin is irregular. Unlike justified text, left justification requires no adjustment to word spacing; the inequities in spacing fall at the end of the lines. The resulting "ragged" right margin adds variety and interest to the page without interfering with legibility.

Left-justified text

Centered text

Right-justified text

Justification of headlines   Titles and headings over left-justified body text should also be flush left. Centered headings pair well with justified text, but justified text should not be used on Web pages. Centered display type contrasts with the asymmetry of the ragged right margin of left-justified body text and produces an unbalanced page.

Justified text, centered head

Left-justified text, centered head

Left-justified text, left-justified head

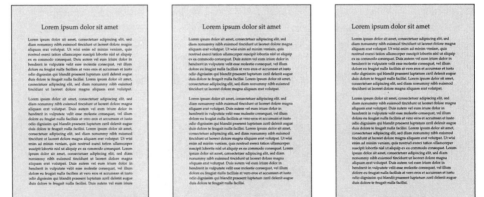

Until typographic options for Web pages become more sophisticated, we recommend that you use left-justified text blocks and headlines as the best solution for most layout situations.

Text on the computer screen is hard to read not only because of the low resolution of computer screens but also because the layout of most Web pages violates a fundamental rule of book and magazine typography: the lines of text on most Web pages are much too long for easy reading. Magazine and book columns are narrow for physiological reasons: at normal reading distances the eye's span of acute focus is only about three inches wide, so designers try to keep dense passages of text in columns not much wider than that comfortable eye span. Wider lines of text require readers to move their heads slightly or strain their eye muscles to track over the long lines of text. Readability suffers because on the long trip back to the left margin the reader may lose track of the next line.

You can use invisible tables (BORDER="0") to restrict the text line length to about fifty to seventy characters per line (see Chapter 4, *Sample page grid*). The exact character count is difficult to predict because of the way different browser software and operating systems display type sizes. In conventional print layouts, columns of thirty to forty characters per line are considered ideal.

We typically use page layout tables with text cells no wider than about 365 pixels. If 12-point Times New Roman type is used, this cell width yields a line about fifty characters long, averaging about nine to ten words per line. We believe this achieves the best balance between space efficiency and legibility. If you are using CSS you can use leading controls to increase line spacing to 15 or 16 points (see *White space*, below). Additional line spacing allows a somewhat longer line length without sacrificing legibility.

CAPITAL AND LOWERCASE LETTERS

Whether you choose uppercase or lowercase letters has a strong effect on the legibility of your headlines. We read primarily by recognizing the overall shape of words, not by parsing each letter and then assembling a recognizable word:

Avoid using all-uppercase headlines. Words formed with capital letters are monotonous rectangles that offer few distinctive shapes to catch the eye:

We recommend downstyle typing (capitalize only the first word and any proper nouns) for your headlines and subheads. Downstyle headlines are more legible, because as we read we primarily scan the tops of words:

Legibility depends on the tops of

Notice how much harder it is to read the bottom half of the same sentence:

Legibility depends on the tops of

If you use initial capital letters in your headlines, you disrupt the reader's scanning of the word forms:

Initial Caps Cause Pointless Bumps

WHITE SPACE

The vertical space in a text block is called leading, and it is the distance from one baseline of text to the next. Leading strongly affects the legibility of text blocks: too much leading makes it hard for the eye to locate the start of the next line, whereas too little leading confuses the lines of type, because the ascenders of one line get jumbled with the descenders of the line above. In plain HTML it is not possible to implement true leading, but CSS offers leading control (referred to as "line spacing" in CSS terminology). In print one general rule is to set the leading of text blocks at about 2 points above the size of the type. For example, 12-point type could be set with 14 points of leading. We suggest generous leading to compensate for the lower resolution of the computer screen, for example, 12-point type with 14 to 16 points of leading.

Indenting paragraphs   There are two major schools of thought on denoting paragraphs. The classic typographic method uses indents to signal the beginning of a new paragraph (as we have in this book). However, many technical, reference, and trade publications now use a blank line of white space to separate paragraphs. Indented paragraphs work especially well for longer blocks of prose, where the indents signal new paragraphs with minimal disruption to the flow of text. Blank line spacing between paragraphs, in contrast, makes a page easy to scan and provides extra white space for visual relief. Either approach is valid as long as the paragraph style is implemented consistently throughout the site.

To indent paragraphs without using CSS, you can insert several non-breaking space characters ( ) at the start of each paragraph. You can also use a transparent single-pixel GIF graphic as a spacer and adjust its horizontal spacing:

```
<IMG SRC="pixel.gif" HEIGHT="1" WIDTH ="1" ALT="" HSPACE="8">
```

If you are using CSS you can set the exact spacing for the indentation using the "text-indent" property of paragraphs.

To separate paragraphs with blank lines you could put a paragraph tag (<P>) at the end of each paragraph. The paragraph tag adds a full blank line between paragraphs. We prefer to use the line break tag (<BR>) followed by a transparent single-pixel GIF graphic as a spacer to achieve better control of the space between paragraphs:

```
<BR>
<IMG SRC="pixel.gif" HEIGHT="1" WIDTH ="1" ALT="" VSPACE="2">
```

TYPEFACES

Each typeface has a unique tone that should produce a harmonious fit between the verbal and visual flow of your content. Until fairly recently, Web authors had no control over typefaces ("fonts" in personal computer terminology). Fonts were set by the browser, so pages were viewed in whatever font the user specified in his or her browser preferences. The more recent versions of HTML allow designers to specify the typeface. This is useful not only for aesthetic reasons but also because of the differing dimensions of typefaces. A layout that is carefully designed using one face may not format correctly in another.

Table set in Palatino

Table set in New York

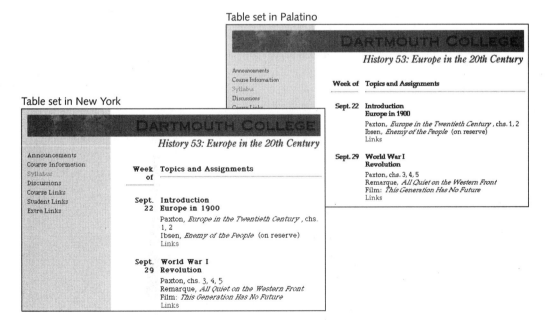

In specifying typefaces you should choose from the resident default fonts for most operating systems. If you specify a font that is not on the user's machine, the browser will display your pages using the user-specified default font. Bear in mind, too, that users can set their browser preferences to ignore font tags and display all pages using their designated default font.

Legibility on screen   Some typefaces are more legible than others on the screen. A traditional typeface such as Times Roman is considered to be one of the most legible on paper, but at screen resolution its size is too small and its shapes look irregular. Screen legibility is most influenced by the x-height (the height of a lowercase "x") and the overall size of the typeface.

Adapted traditional typefaces   Times New Roman is a good example of a traditional typeface that has been adapted for use on computer screens. A serif typeface like Times New Roman (the default text face in most Web browsers) is about average in legibility on the computer screen, with a moderate x-height. Times New Roman is a good font to use in text-heavy documents that will probably be printed by readers rather than read from the screen. The compact letter size of Times New Roman also makes it a good choice if you need to pack a lot of words into a small space.

Designed for the screen   Typefaces such as Georgia and Verdana were designed specifically for legibility on the computer screen; they have exaggerated x-heights and are very large compared to more traditional typefaces in the same point size. These fonts offer excellent legibility for Web pages designed to be read directly from the screen. However, the exaggerated x-heights and heavy letterforms of these fonts look massive and clumsy when transferred to the high-resolution medium of paper.

Choosing typefaces   The most conventional scheme for using typefaces is to use a serif face such as Times New Roman or Georgia for body text and a sans serif face such as Verdana or Arial as a contrast for headlines. We generally set our text-laden Web pages in Times New Roman because it produces a reasonable balance between density of information and overall legibility. Most readers expect a serif font for long blocks of text and find Times New Roman comfortable to read off-screen from paper printouts.

Various studies purport to show that serif type is more legible than sans serif type and vice versa. You can truly judge type legibility only within the context of the situation – on the screen – as users will see your Web page.

Specifying typefaces in HTML   The FACE attribute of the FONT tag allows you to specify any typeface, but many computers only have the default operating system fonts installed. The most useful fonts that ship with the Apple Macintosh and Microsoft Windows95 operating systems are reproduced here (we have omitted bitmap fonts and decorative or novelty typefaces):

Windows95

Times New Roman

Each typeface has a unique tone that should produce a harmonious fit between the verbal and visual flow of your content.

Georgia

Each typeface has a unique tone that should produce a harmonious fit between the verbal and visual flow of your content.

Verdana

Each typeface has a unique tone that should produce a harmonious fit between the verbal and visual flow of your content.

Arial

Each typeface has a unique tone that should produce a harmonious fit between the verbal and visual flow of your content.

Trebuchet

Each typeface has a unique tone that should produce a harmonious fit between the verbal and visual flow of your content.

Macintosh

Times New Roman

Each typeface has a unique tone that should produce a harmonious fit between the verbal and visual flow of your content.

Georgia

Each typeface has a unique tone that should produce a harmonious fit between the verbal and visual flow of your content.

Verdana

Each typeface has a unique tone that should produce a harmonious fit between the verbal and visual flow of your content.

Arial

Each typeface has a unique tone that should produce a harmonious fit between the verbal and visual flow of your content.

Trebuchet

Each typeface has a unique tone that should produce a harmonious fit between the verbal and visual flow of your content.

You may use either a variation of the serif font or a contrasting sans serif face for the display type. It is safest to use a single typographic family and vary its weight and size for display type and emphasis. If you do choose to combine serif and sans serif faces, select fonts that are compatible and don't use more than two typefaces (one serif, one sans serif) on a page. If the typeface you specify is not available on the user's computer, the browser will switch to the default font (generally "Times New Roman" or "Times"). To increase the chances that the reader will see a typeface you are happy with, you can specify multiple fonts in the FACE attribute. The browser will check for the presence of each font (in the order given), so you can specify three or four alternates before the browser applies the default font.

```
<FONT FACE="Verdana, Geneva, Arial, Helvetica">Typefaces</FONT>
```

If you are using both tables and font tags in your document, the combination can produce unpredictable results. The TABLE tag is not allowed inside a FONT tag, which means that the text inside table cells will display in the default font set by the browser. To apply your font settings to text inside tables you must include the font settings *within each table cell:*

```
<TD>
<FONT FACE="Arial, Geneva, Verdana, Helvetica">Typefaces</FONT>
</TD>
```

A good way to make sure that your type settings are functioning correctly is to set your browser's default proportional font setting to something that is obviously different from your intended font. For example, set your browser's default font to Courier if you are not specifying Courier in your page font tags. When you view your page, anything that appears in Courier must not be contained within a proper FONT FACE tag.

EMPHASIS

A Web page of solid body text is hard to scan for content structure and will not engage the eye. Adding display type to a document will provide landmarks to direct the reader through your content. Display type establishes an information structure and adds visual variety to draw the reader into your material. The key to effective display type is the careful and economic use of typographic emphasis.

There are time-honored typographical devices for adding emphasis to a block of text, but be sure to use them sparingly. If you make everything bold, then nothing will stand out and it will seem as if you are **shouting** at your readers. A good rule of thumb when working with type is to add emphasis using one parameter at a time. If you want to draw attention to the section heads in your document, don't set them large, bold, and all caps. If you want them to be larger, increase their size by one measure. If you prefer bold, leave the heads the same size as your body text and make them bold. You will soon discover that only a small variation is required to establish visual contrast.

Italics   Italicized text attracts the eye because it contrasts in shape from body text. Use italics for convention – when listing book or periodical titles, for example – or within text for stressed or foreign words or phrases. Avoid setting large blocks of text in italics because the readability of italicized text, particularly at screen resolutions, is much lower than in comparably sized roman text.

Bold   Boldface text gives emphasis because it contrasts in color from the body text. Section subheads work well set in bold. Boldface text is readable on screen, though large blocks of text set in bold lack contrast and therefore lose their effectiveness.

Underlined   Underlined text is a carryover from the days of the typewriter, when such options as italics and boldface were unavailable. In addition to its aesthetic shortcomings (too heavy, interferes with letter shapes), underlining has a special functional meaning in Web documents. Most readers have their browser preferences set to underline links. This default browser setting ensures that people with monochromatic monitors or people who are color-blind can identify links within text blocks. If you include underlined text on your Web page it will certainly be confused with a hypertext link.

Colored text   Although the use of color is another option for differentiating type, colored text, like underlining, has a special functional meaning in Web documents. You should avoid putting colored text within text blocks because readers will assume that the colored text is a hypertext link and click on it. Colored text does work well as a subtle means to distinguish section heads, however. Choose dark shades of color that contrast with the page background, and avoid using colors close to the default Web link colors of blue and violet.

Capital letters   Capitalized text is one of the most common and least effective methods for adding typographical emphasis. We recognize words in two ways, by parsing letter groups and by recognizing word shapes. Words or headlines set in all capital letters form rectangles with no distinctive shape. To read a block of text set in all capital letters we must parse the letter groups – read the text letter by letter – which is uncomfortable and significantly slows reading. As you read the following paragraph, notice how tiring the process is:

> THE DESIGN OF THE SITE WILL DETERMINE THE ORGANIZATIONAL FRAMEWORK OF YOUR WEB SITE. AT THIS STAGE YOU WILL MAKE THE ESSENTIAL DECISIONS ABOUT WHAT YOUR AUDIENCE WANTS FROM YOU, WHAT YOU WISH TO SAY, AND HOW TO ARRANGE THE CONTENT TO BEST MEET YOUR AUDIENCE'S NEEDS. ALTHOUGH PEOPLE WILL INSTANTLY NOTICE THE GRAPHIC DESIGN OF YOUR WEB PAGES, THE ORGANIZATION OF THE SITE WILL HAVE THE GREATEST IMPACT ON THEIR EXPERIENCE.

Spacing and indentation   One of the most effective and subtle ways to vary the visual contrast and relative importance of a piece of text is simply to isolate it or treat it differently from the surrounding text. If you want your major headers to stand out more without making them larger, add space before the header to separate it from any previous copy, and then add some space just after the title to differentiate it from the text block that follows:

```
<IMG SRC="pixel.gif" HEIGHT="1" WIDTH ="1" ALT="" VSPACE="10"><BR>
Sample title line with extra spacing<BR>
<IMG SRC="pixel.gif" HEIGHT="1" WIDTH ="1" ALT="" VSPACE="1"><BR>
```

Indentation is another effective means of distinguishing bulleted lists, quotations, or example text (such as the capitalization example above). HTML lists are automatically indented (too far, in our estimation), and you can use the BLOCKQUOTE tag to indent blocks of text.

CONSISTENCY

As in traditional print publishing, high-quality Web sites adhere to established type style settings consistently throughout the site. Consistency gives polish to a site and encourages visitors to stay by creating an expectation about the structure of a text. If this expectation is confounded by sloppy, inconsistent formatting, you will confuse your readers and they may not return.

You should decide on such settings as fonts, inter-paragraph spacing, the size of subheads, and so on and then create a written style guide to help you maintain these settings as you develop the site. This step is especially critical for large sites that incorporate numerous pages.

Cascading Style Sheets to manage consistency   If you choose to use CSS you will have powerful tools to maintain the consistency of styles throughout your site. This is particularly true if you opt to use a master style sheet for your whole site via the "Link" option in CSS (see *Cascading Style Sheets*, below).

CROSS-PLATFORM ISSUES

RELATIVE FONT SIZES

The Macintosh and Windows operating systems display type differently, even when the same typefaces are being used. In general, type displayed on Windows Web browsers will look 2 to 3 points larger than the equivalent face on the Macintosh. Thus a line of 12-point Times type on a Macintosh looks more like 14 points in Times New Roman on a Windows machine. This difference in font rendering can have a big impact on your page layouts. The table on the facing page shows the major Microsoft TrueType typefaces in their 12-point sizes, as displayed in both Windows and on a Macintosh.

If you don't have ready access to a machine with "the other" operating system and you use Netscape Navigator, you can use Netscape's "Preferences/Fonts" box to change the default text size from 12 to 14 (Mac users) or from 12 to 11 or 10 (Windows users). If you use Internet Explorer you can use the "Larger" or "Smaller" controls on the button bar to manipulate the default font size of the text.

Windows95

Arial
Courier
Georgia
Times New Roman
Trebuchet MS
Verdana

Macintosh OS 8

Arial
Courier
Georgia
Times New Roman
Trebuchet
Verdana

FONT FACES

The basic fonts that come with Windows95 and the Macintosh operating system are listed below. If you are going to use the FACE attribute to specify type, you should probably stick to the typefaces listed here, and you should always specify at least one typeface from each operating system (for example: "Arial, Geneva") to avoid having the browser render your pages in the default font:

Windows95

Arial
Courier
Courier New
MS Sans Serif
MS Serif
Times New Roman
Verdana

Macintosh OS 8

Charcoal
Chicago
Courier
Geneva
Helvetica
Monaco
New York
Palatino
Times

Remember that many Macintosh users who have installed Microsoft Office or Microsoft's Internet Explorer Web browser will have "Windows" fonts installed on their systems. If you specify the fonts "Georgia, Times" in your FONT tags, many Macintosh users will see their text set in Georgia, just as Windows users do.

Also note in the relative font sizes example above that although "Trebuchet" and "Trebuchet MS" are basically the same typeface, the exact name you specify in the FACE attribute matters. If you want both Macintosh and Windows95 users to see the typeface Trebuchet, then use both names in your FACE attribute tags:

<FONT FACE="Trebuchet, Trebuchet MS">Names matter</FONT>

CASCADING STYLE SHEETS

This book is not a manual on HTML, and covering the full design implications of Cascading Style Sheets (CSS) is well beyond the scope of this chapter. However, if you are not using CSS to manage the graphic design of your Web site, you should at least be planning a transition to CSS technology in the next year or two. Here is a brief outline of the rationale behind CSS, pointing out some of the implications for managers of large enterprise Web or intranet sites.

ADVANTAGES OF CSS

Cascading Style Sheets offer Web designers two key advantages in managing complex Web sites:

Separation of content and design   CSS gives site developers the best of both worlds: content markup that reflects the logical structure of the information and the freedom to specify exactly how each HTML tag will look.

Efficient control over large document sets   The most powerful implementations of CSS will allow site designers to control the graphic "look and feel" of thousands of pages by modifying a single master style sheet document.

HOW STYLE SHEETS WORK

Style sheets are not new. Every graphic Web browser (even back to Mosaic 1.0) has used style sheets. It just wasn't possible to modify the fixed styles that browsers used to determine, for example, exactly how H1 headers look on the screen. The fundamental idea behind CSS is to let site authors and users determine the size, style, and layout details for each standard HTML tag.

If you have ever used the "styles" features of a page layout or word processing program, you will understand the basic idea behind CSS. The styles feature of a word processor is used to determine exactly how your titles, subheadings, and body copy will look, and then the copy is formatted when you apply a style to each element. Once all the copy has been styled, you can change the look of each occurrence of every element just by changing the style information. CSS works in the same way, except that with CSS you can set up one master style sheet that will control the visual styling of every page in your site that is linked to the master style sheet:

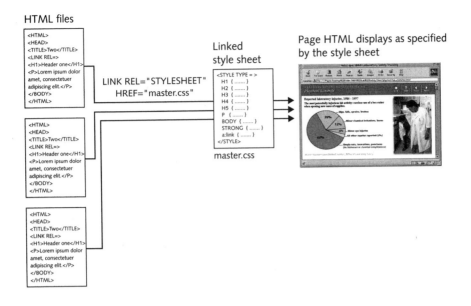

HTML files

Linked
style sheet

Page HTML displays as specified
by the style sheet

LINK REL="STYLESHEET"
HREF="master.css"

master.css

At this writing (late 1998), css remains a terrific idea whose time has not yet come for most users. Current versions (4.x) of Netscape Navigator and Internet Explorer do not fully implement the most recent World Wide Web Consortium (w3c) specification for css, and the two dominant browsers do not render css pages in identical ways. But Cascading Style Sheets are the "elephant in the living room" for Web designers and managers of enterprise Web sites – css is too big an issue to ignore. Right now most major Web site managers are taking a watchful "wait-and-see" attitude on the subject, and we agree that for many this is currently the smart move.

If, however, you are planning to establish a large collection of intranet documents (such as personnel policies and procedures) for an enterprise, the immediate advantages of shifting to css may well outweigh the temporary struggles with current browsers. In such large systems, you should avoid any HTML tags aimed solely at improving the visual display of your pages and adhere closely to "plain-vanilla" HTML while letting style sheets handle the graphic design issues.

TYPE GRAPHICS

Typography cannot always be neatly separated from the graphics of your Web site. Graphic text can be tightly integrated with images in ways that are impossible in HTML text:

For aesthetic reasons you may choose to use graphical representations of type rather than manipulate HTML type. In either case you'll need to understand how to best render type within GIF (Graphics Interchange Format) and JPEG (Joint Photographic Experts Group) graphics.

ANTIALIASED TYPE

Antialiasing is a technique widely used in computer graphics to optimize the look of graphics and typography on the display screen. Antialiasing visually "smoothes" the shapes in graphics and type by inserting pixels of intermediate colors along boundary edges between colors. In typography, antialiasing removes the jagged edges of larger type characters. At normal viewing distances antialiasing gives the impression that the type is rendered at a higher resolution:

Not antialiased   Antialiased

Creating antialiased type Sophisticated image editing programs such as Adobe Photoshop will create antialiased type automatically, and these "paint" image editors are where most Web designers create their graphic typography. If, however, you have a complex arrangement of typography and graphics (say, for a home page banner), you may wish to work first in a drawing program such as Adobe Illustrator or Macromedia FreeHand. Drawing programs are better at laying out text and will let you edit the text up to the final rendering into a paint (GIF or JPEG) graphic to use on the Web page. Final rendering is usually done by importing the graphic into Photoshop, where all text will automatically become antialiased:

Bitmap photo in Adobe Illustrator, with Postscript lettering for major headers

It's often better to do this kind of layout in a drawing program such as Adobe Illustrator, where the text can be easily edited

The composite menu graphic is imported into Adobe Photoshop, where the typography becomes antialiased

Composited bitmap, saved as a progressive JPEG

We often use graphic type within banner or navigational graphics, but we rarely use graphic type simply as a stylistic substitute for headlines or subheads within a Web page. Purely graphic typography cannot be searched and indexed along with the HTML-based text on a Web page. Your best option is to repeat the textual content of the graphic inside an ALT tag and hope that search engines will pick up that content, too. Finally, bear in mind that graphic type is far more difficult to edit or update than HTML text.

When not to use antialiasing   Antialiasing is great for large display type, but it is not suitable for small type sizes, especially type smaller than 10 points. The antialiasing reduces the legibility of small type, particularly when you import it into Photoshop from a drawing program like Adobe Illustrator. If you need to antialias small type sizes, do it in Photoshop:

Geneva	Search	Home	Comments	Index	
Arial	Search	Home	Comments	Index	Type not antialiased Set in Microsoft Word and captured as a screen grab
Times New Roman	Search	Home	Comments	Index	
Georgia	Search	Home	Comments	Index	

Geneva	Search	Home	Comments	Index	
Arial	Search	Home	Comments	Index	Type set in Adobe Illustrator and imported into Adobe Photoshop with antialiasing on (Results are poor for small type sizes; avoid doing this)
Times New Roman	Search	Home	Comments	Index	
Georgia	Search	Home	Comments	Index	

Geneva	**Search**	**Home**	**Comments**	**Index**	
Arial	**Search**	**Home**	**Comments**	**Index**	Type set in Adobe Photoshop with antialiasing on Best results for small antialiased type sizes
Times New Roman	Search	Home	Comments	Index	
Georgia	**Search**	**Home**	**Comments**	**Index**	

For the anatomic illustration below we used non-antialiased 9-point Geneva (a Macintosh screen font) for the illustration labels:

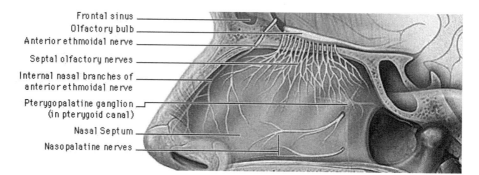

Frontal sinus
Olfactory bulb
Anterior ethmoidal nerve
Septal olfactory nerves
Internal nasal branches of anterior ethmoidal nerve
Pterygopalatine ganglion (in pterygoid canal)
Nasal Septum
Nasopalatine nerves

6 *Editorial Style*

Prefer the specific to the general, the definite to the vague,
the concrete to the abstract.
– William Strunk, Jr., and E. B. White, *The Elements of Style*

WEB PAGES have many similarities to individual pages in print publications, but because they may be accessed directly without preamble, Web pages must be more independent than print pages. Too many Web pages end up as isolated fragments of information, divorced from the larger context of their parent Web sites through the lack of essential links and the simpler failure to inform the reader properly of their contents.

WRITING STYLE FOR ONLINE DOCUMENTS

Writing for the Web is a new medium with no definitive guide or set of standards. One popular school of thought holds that Web readers want to see as little text as possible and are opposed to long documents and the physical act of scrolling. This may have been true when the Web was a technological novelty and most Web "surfers" were looking for a free-form, associative experience with the variety of content on the Internet. Now people are becoming impatient with slogging though masses of insubstantial material to get what they are seeking: information. Clear, concise, complete, accurate information.

One of the most obvious characteristics of Web writing is hypertext links. Web authors use hypertext links to create or supplement concepts: a list of related links can reinforce their content or even serve as the focus of their site. The problem posed by links has little to do with the Web but is rooted in the concept of hypertext: Can the quick juxtaposition of two separate but conceptually related pieces of information encourage a better understanding of the overall message? A collection of links cannot create or sustain an argument or deliver a collection of facts as efficiently or legibly as conventional linear prose. When there is no sustained narrative, readers are sent aimlessly wandering in their quest for information. Links also become a maintenance issue, because most Web pages are ephemeral. Broken links shake the reader's confidence in the validity and timeliness of content. Links should be used sparingly and as a reinforcement of, not a substitute for, content.

Organizing your prose   Documents written to be read online must be concise and structured for scanning. People tend to skim Web pages rather than read them word by word. Use headings, lists, and typographical emphasis for words or sections you wish to highlight; these are the elements that will grab the user's attention during a quick scan. Keep these elements clear and precise – use your page and section heads to describe the material. The "inverted pyramid" style used in journalism works well on Web pages, with the conclusion appearing at the beginning of a text. Place the important facts near the top of the first paragraph where users can find them quickly.

That said, keep in mind that much content is not well suited to the telegraphic style that works well for online documents. Web authors often cut so much out of their presentations that what remains would barely fill a printed pamphlet. Concise writing is always better, but don't "dumb down" what you have to say. You can assume that readers will print anything longer than half a page and read it offline. Simply make printing easy for your readers and you can use the Web to deliver content without cutting the heart out of what you have to say.

Another way to style online documents is to break up your information into logical "chunks" connected by hypertext links, but only where it makes sense (see Chapter 3, *"Chunking" information*). Don't break up a long document arbitrarily; users will have to download each segment and will have difficulty printing or saving the entire piece. The key to good chunking is to divide your information into comprehensive segments. That way readers will have direct and complete access to the topics they are interested in without having to wade through irrelevant material or follow a series of links to get the whole picture.

PROSE STYLE FOR THE WEB

Our writing style example below explains the steps involved in creating a successful Web site. The first style is vague and verbose. The second is concise: we simply list the facts. It is this second writing style that is most suitable for Web documents. Most Web readers are looking for information, and they find it not by reading a Web page word by word but rather by scanning the page for relevant items.

Vague and verbose   You must read every word in this paragraph in order to understand the steps involved in creating Web sites:

> Web site development is a complex process that involves many steps and tasks that range from budgeting to design and evaluation. First, you need to define the scope of your project and determine a budget for site development. Then you need to survey and map the structure of your information. The next step is to establish a look and feel for your site, and then comes the actual construction of your site. Once your site is finished you need to make sure people know that it's there

and how to find it. Finally, you should spend time evaluating your site's effectiveness. As you embark on the process of developing a Web site, keep these steps in mind and make sure that you have the organizational backing, budget, and personnel you need to make the project a success.

Concise and factual   In this version, we turned the wordy explanation of the process into a concise list of steps to follow:

The process of developing a Web site generally follows these steps:

1 Site definition and budgeting
2 Information architecture
3 Site design
4 Site construction
5 Site marketing
6 Tracking and evaluation

Before beginning to develop a Web site, make sure you have the organizational backing, budget, and personnel you need to perform these steps successfully.

TITLES AND SUBTITLES

Editorial landmarks like titles and headers are the fundamental human interface device in Web pages, just as they are in any print publication. A consistent approach to titles, headlines, and subheadings in your documents will help your readers navigate through a complex set of Web pages.

TEXT STYLES
The text styles we recommend:

Headline style: Bold, capitalize initial letters of words
• Document titles
• References to other Web sites
• Titles of documents mentioned in the text
• Proper names, product names, trade names

Down style: Bold, capitalize first word only
• Subheads
• References to other sections within the site
• Figure titles
• Lists

Web page titles are designated in the HTML document head section with the TITLE tag. The title is crucial for two reasons: it is often the first thing users with slow Internet connections will see and it becomes the text for any bookmarks the reader makes to your pages. The page title should:

- Incorporate the name of your company, organization, or Web site
- Form a concise, plainly worded reminder of the page contents

Always consider what your page title will look like in a long list of bookmarks. Will the title remind the reader of what he or she found interesting about your pages?

TEXT FORMATTING FOR WEB DOCUMENTS

Some points about text formatting specific to the Web:

Excessive markup   Beware of too much markup in your paragraphs. Too many links or too many styles of typeface will destroy the homogeneous, even "type color" that characterizes good typesetting.

Link colors   If you are including links in the body of your text, choose custom link colors that closely match your text color. Reading from the screen is hard enough without struggling with distracting links colors scattered across the page.

Use the best tool   Write your text in a good word processing program with spell-checking and search features. Transfer your text to HTML only after it has been proofread.

Style sheets in word processors   Don't use the word processor's style sheets to produce "All capitals" or other formatting effects. You will lose those special formats when you convert to plain ASCII text for HTML use.

Special characters   Don't use the "smart quotes" feature. Avoid all special characters, such as bullets, ligatures, and typographer's en and em dashes, that are not supported in standard HTML text. Consult a good HTML guide book (we recommend several in the References) for the listing of special and international characters supported through HTML's extended character formatting.

No auto hyphens   Never use the automatic hyphenation feature of your word processor on text destined for the Web. This may add nonstandard "optional hyphen" characters that will not display properly in Web browsers.

LINKS

Two basic types of links are used in Web sites: navigational links connect pages within a site and the classic hypertext links offer parenthetical material, footnotes, digressions, or parallel themes that the author believes will enrich the main content of the page. Although navigational links can cause problems in site design, more disruptive is the overuse or poor placement of hypertext links.

Hypertext links pose two fundamental design problems. They disrupt the flow of content in your site by inviting the reader to leave your site. They can also radically alter the context of information by dumping the reader into unfamiliar territory without preamble or explanation.

The primary design strategy in thoughtful hypertext is to use links to reinforce your message, not to distract readers or send them off chasing a minor footnote in some other Web site. Most links in a Web site should point to other resources *within* your Web site, pages that share the same graphic design, navigational controls, and overall content theme. Whenever possible, integrate related visuals or text materials into your site so that readers do not have the sense that you have dumped them outside the framework of your site. If you must send your reader away, make sure the material around the link makes it clear that the reader will be leaving your Web site and entering another site by following the link.

MAINTAIN CONTEXT

The key to good hypertext linking is to *maintain context*, so that the reader stays within the narrative flow and design environment of your site. If you place a simple link on your page, these plain links will work within a single browser window – your content will disappear and the linked page will fill the window. If you use this kind of link to point away from your site, you will probably lose your readers.

The simplest way to maintain context using links to other sites is to add the TARGET="main" argument to your link tags. This will cause the linked page to appear in a new browser window in front of the one containing your page. This feature allows your reader to access new material without losing visual contact with your site.

Frames offer a more complex way to maintain narrative and design context. Using frames you can split the browser screen between your site and the material you wish to bring up with a link. Frames allow you to supply commentary on material in another site and also to maintain navigation links back to your site (see Chapter 4, *Frames*).

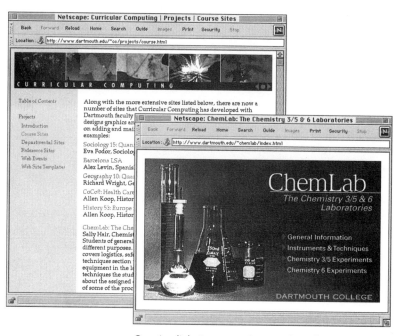

Opening links in a secondary window allows users to explore related material without losing contact with your site

PLACING LINKS

Links are a <u>distraction.</u> It is pointless to <u>write</u> <u>a</u> <u>paragraph</u> and then fill it with <u>invitations</u> to your <u>reader</u> to go <u>elsewhere.</u> You can minimize the disruptive quality of links by managing their placement on the page. Put only the most salient links within the body of your text, and remember that these links should open new browser windows so that you don't supplant the original pages. But most links do not belong in the middle of the page – they won't be important enough to justify the potential distractions they pose. Group all minor, illustrative, parenthetic, or footnote links at the bottom of the document where they are available but not distracting.

If you do place links in the body of your text, pay close attention to your language. Never construct a sentence around a link phrase, such as "click here for more information." Write the sentence as you normally would, and place the link anchor on the most relevant word in the sentence.

- Poor: <u>Click here</u> for more information on placing links within your text.
- Better: Web links are powerful but can cause problems if they are <u>placed carelessly.</u>

7 *Web Graphics*

Who are you gonna believe, me or your own eyes?
– Groucho Marx

IN THIS CHAPTER we show you techniques to optimize the look and efficiency of your Web page graphics. Although electronic publishing frees you from the cost and limitations of color reproduction on paper, you will still need to make careful calculations (and a few compromises) if you wish to optimize your graphics and photographs for various display monitors and Internet access speeds.

CHARACTERISTICS OF WEB GRAPHICS

The parameters that influence the display of Web graphics are the user's display monitor and bandwidth capacity. Much of the Web audience accesses the Internet via modem and views Web pages on monitors that display only 256 colors. This reality imposes limits on the size of files and number of colors that can be included in Web graphics.

COLOR DISPLAYS

Color monitors for desktop microcomputers are based on cathode ray tubes (CRTS). Because CRTS transmit light, CRT displays use the red-green-blue (RGB) additive color model. The RGB model is called "additive" because a combination of the three pure colors red, green, and blue "adds up" to white light:

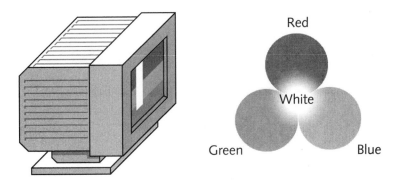

The computer's operating system organizes the display screen into a grid of x and y coordinates, like a checkerboard. Each little box on the screen is called a "pixel" (short for "picture element"). Current Macintosh and Windows displays are composed of these grids of pixels.

Pixels and color depth   To control the color of each pixel on the screen, the operating system must dedicate a small amount of memory to each pixel. In aggregate this memory dedicated to the display screen is often referred to as "video RAM" or "VRAM" (Video Random Access Memory). In the simplest form of black-and-white computer displays, a single bit of memory is assigned to each pixel. Because each memory bit is either positive or negative (0 or 1), a 1-bit display system can manage only two colors (black or white) for each pixel on the screen:

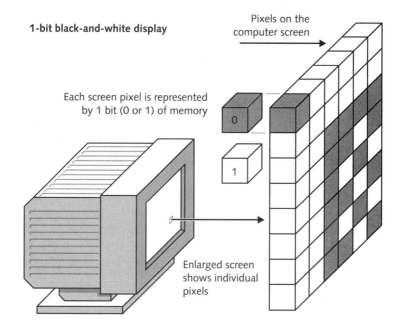

1-bit black-and-white display

Pixels on the computer screen

Each screen pixel is represented by 1 bit (0 or 1) of memory

0

1

Enlarged screen shows individual pixels

If more bits of memory are dedicated to each pixel in the display, more colors can be managed. When 8 bits of memory are dedicated to each pixel, each pixel could be one of 256 colors. (256 = 2 to the eighth power; in other words, 256 is the maximum number of unique combinations of zeros and ones you can make with 8 bits.) This kind of computer display is called an "8-bit" or "256-color" display, and is common in current microcomputing, especially on laptop computers and older desktop machines. Although the exact colors that an 8-bit screen can display are not fixed, there can never be more than 256 unique colors on the screen at once:

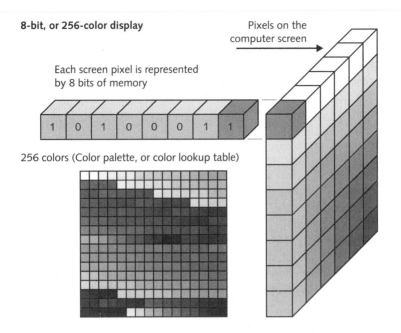

8-bit, or 256-color display

Pixels on the computer screen

Each screen pixel is represented by 8 bits of memory

| 1 | 0 | 1 | 0 | 0 | 0 | 1 | 1 |

256 colors (Color palette, or color lookup table)

If still more memory is dedicated to each pixel, nearly photographic color is achievable on the computer screen. "True-color" or "24-bit" color displays can show millions of unique colors simultaneously on the computer screen. True-color images are composed by dedicating 24 bits of memory to each pixel; 8 each for the red, green, and blue components ($8 + 8 + 8 = 24$):

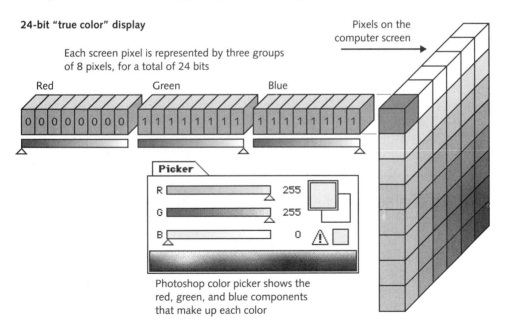

24-bit "true color" display

Pixels on the computer screen

Each screen pixel is represented by three groups of 8 pixels, for a total of 24 bits

Red   Green   Blue

| 0 | 0 | 0 | 0 | 0 | 0 | 0 | 0 | 1 | 1 | 1 | 1 | 1 | 1 | 1 | 1 | 1 | 1 | 1 | 1 | 1 | 1 | 1 | 1 |

Picker

R   255
G   255
B   0

Photoshop color picker shows the red, green, and blue components that make up each color

The amount of VRAM dedicated to each screen pixel in the display is commonly referred to as the "color depth" of the monitor. Most Macintosh and Windows microcomputers sold in recent years can display color depths greater than 8-bit, in thousands (16-bit) or millions (24-bit) of simultaneous colors. Many computer users, however, are either not aware that they can set their displays to show more colors or use software that requires an 8-bit display (such as many computer games). To check your computer system for the range of color depths available to you, use the "Display" control panel (Windows) or the "Monitors" control panel (Macintosh):

Windows95, NT

Macintosh

Color depth and graphics files   The terminology and memory schemes used in color displays are directly analogous to those used to describe color depth in graphics files. In their uncompressed states, 8-bit, or 256-color, image files

256-color palette

dedicate 8 bits to each color pixel in the image. In 8-bit images the 256 colors that make up the image are stored in an array called a "palette" or an "index." The color palette may also be referred to as a "color lookup table" (CLUT). As mentioned above, 8-bit images can never contain more than 256 unique colors.

True-color, or 24-bit, images are typically much larger than 8-bit images in their uncompressed state, because 24 bits of memory are dedicated to each pixel, typically arranged in three monochrome layers – red, green, and blue:

"BROWSER-SAFE" COLORS

The color management system currently used by Web browser software is based on an 8-bit, 216-color (not 256) palette. The browser-safe color palette is a solution devised by Netscape to solve the problem of displaying color graphics in a similar way on many kinds of display screens, with browsers running under different operating systems (such as Macintosh, Windows, and UNIX). Because a majority of the Web audience several years ago had 8-bit display screens, 256 colors was the upper limit for the color palette. But the various versions of the Windows operating system (which currently represent about 95 percent of the microcomputer market) reserve 40 colors for displaying such graphic interface elements as windows, menus, screen wallpaper, icons, and buttons, which leaves just 216 colors to display everything else. The 216 colors chosen by Netscape are identical in both the Macintosh and Windows system palettes. Although the browser-safe color scheme originated at Netscape, at present both of the dominant Web browsers (Netscape Navigator and Microsoft Internet Explorer) use the same color management system.

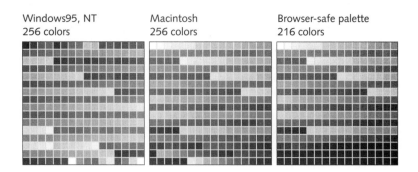

Windows95, NT 256 colors	Macintosh 256 colors	Browser-safe palette 216 colors

DITHERING

Full-color photographs may contain an almost infinite range of color values. *Dithering* is the most common means of reducing the color range of images down to the 256 (or fewer) colors seen in 8-bit GIF images.

Dithering is the process of juxtaposing pixels of two colors to create the illusion that a third color is present. A simple example is an image with only black and white in the color palette. By combining black and white pixels in complex patterns a graphics program like Adobe Photoshop can create the illusion of gray values:

Full-color image
dithered
to two colors

The same process softens the effect of reducing the number of colors in full-color images:

Original full-color photograph   Dithered to 256 colors

Most images are dithered in a diffusion or randomized pattern to diminish the harsh transition from one color to another. But dithering also reduces the overall sharpness of an image, and it often introduces a noticeable grainy pattern in the image. This loss of image detail is especially apparent when full-color photos are dithered down to the 216-color "browser-safe" palette:

Original full-tone image

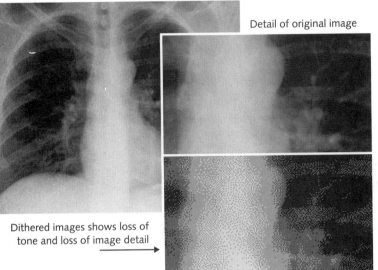

Detail of original image

Dithered images shows loss of
tone and loss of image detail

Dithering done by the browser If a reader of your Web site has his or her display monitor set to 256 colors, then the Web browser will display images using the 216-color browser-safe color palette. In this situation there is no way to force the browser to display a color outside the browser-safe palette. If any of your photographs, graphic design elements, or background colors use hues outside the browser-safe palette, the Web browser will automatically dither the displayed images into the browser-safe colors. The effect of using "unsafe" colors for your major graphic elements is that readers with 256-color displays will see a lot of heavily dithered images. This may be acceptable for some visual elements on the page, but if your basic navigation buttons and background graphics are dithered, parts of the page will be hard to read and the overall effect will be amateurish:

Navigation graphics done in
browser-safe colors

Graphics not done in browser-safe
colors dither on 256-color screens

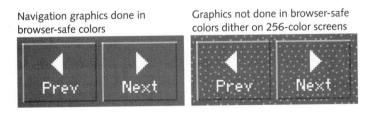

Coping with browser-safe colors   The browser-safe palette is restrictive, but there are so many users who still set their monitors to 256 colors that you must consider how your designs will look on those screens. Not every image on your page needs to be in browser-safe colors, however. You may choose to use GIF graphics with custom colors or full-color JPEG graphics and just accept that they will dither on some screens. The best strategy is usually to mix navigation graphics in browser-safe colors with full-color JPEG graphics. The full-color images will be dithered on 256-color screens, but the navigation buttons will look the same on all screens.

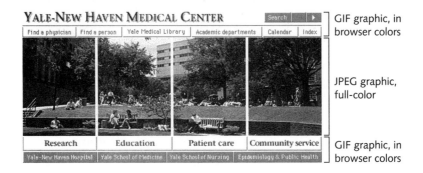

GIF graphic, in
browser colors

JPEG graphic,
full-color

GIF graphic, in
browser colors

SCREEN RESOLUTION

Screen resolution refers to the number of pixels a screen can display within a given area. Screen resolution is usually expressed in pixels per linear inch of screen. Most personal computers displays have resolutions that vary from 72 to 96 pixels per inch (ppi). The resolution of the display screen is dependent on how the monitor and display card are configured, but it's safe to assume that most users fall into the lower end of the range, or about 72 to 80 ppi.

Images destined for print can be created at various resolutions, but images for Web pages are always limited by the resolution of the computer screen. Thus a square GIF graphic of 72 by 72 pixels will be approximately one inch square on a 72-ppi display monitor. When you are creating graphics for Web pages you should always use the 1:1 display ratio (one pixel in the image equals one pixel on the screen), because this is how big the image will display on the Web page. Images that are too large should be reduced to display at proper size at a resolution of 72 ppi.

GAMMA

In computer imaging and display screens "gamma" refers to the degree of contrast between the midlevel gray values of an image. The technical explanations of gamma are irrelevant here – the visual effect of changing gamma values is easy to see. If you own a copy of Adobe Photoshop, open an image with an average range of colors and contrasts and use the "Levels" control to change the gamma settings (see the Photoshop manual for details). Images will change noticeably with even minor changes in gamma settings. Gamma considerations are particularly important if you are displaying images with very long gray scales (such as medical diagnostic images and fine black-and-white photography) or images in which the exact color values are critical (such as works of art and clinical medical photographs):

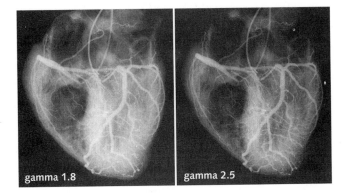

The default gamma settings for Macintosh (1.8 target gamma) and Windows (2.5 target gamma) monitors are quite different, and this can lead to unpleasant surprises when you first see your images displayed on "the other" platform. Mac users will see darker and more contrasting images on Windows displays; Windows users will see flat and washed-out images on Mac displays. Most Web designers opt for a middle-ground solution, lightening images slightly if they work on the Macintosh; darkening slightly and adding a little contrast if they work in Windows.

If you use Adobe Photoshop on a Macintosh you can use the "Gamma" control panel that ships with Photoshop to experiment with your monitor's gamma settings. To simulate the Windows display, set the target gamma to 2.2 and the gamma adjustment slider to "−43," then save those settings.

In the Windows version of Photoshop, the gamma control applies only to images within Photoshop windows, not to the global display environment as it does on the Macintosh. The default gamma setting for the Windows version of Photoshop is 1.8 (the same as on the Mac). To see how your graphics might look once they are out of Photoshop and into your Windows Web browser, use the gamma control in Windows Photoshop to boost the Photoshop display gamma to 2.5 (to match the normal Windows operating system gamma). As the Portable Network Graphics (PNG) image format (see the description below) becomes more popular, the problem of differing gamma values should be solved because PNG images can automatically adjust to differing display gamma values.

Most Web users currently access their Internet service providers via 28.8 kilobits per second (kbps) modems from their homes, offices, or remote work sites. At 28.8 kbps the actual download rate is only about 3.6 kilobytes (KB) per second (8 bits make a byte). This means that a modest 36 KB graphic on your Web page could take ten seconds or longer to load into the reader's Web browser. Actual data transmission rates will vary depending on the user's modem, Web server speed, Internet connection, and other factors, but the overall point is clear: the more graphics you incorporate, the longer the reader will have to wait to see your page. A full-screen graphic menu on your home page plus background graphics could leave your modem-based readers twiddling their thumbs for a full minute or more, even if they have a state-of-the-art modem and a good Internet connection. Look at your watch (better yet, hold your breath) for a full minute, then decide whether you're willing to ask your users to wait this long when they visit your Web site.

A better strategy is to increase the graphics loading of your pages gradually, drawing users into your site with reasonable download times. As readers become more engaged with your content, they will be more willing to endure longer delays, especially if you give them notes about the size of graphics or warnings that particular pages are full of graphics and will take longer to download. At today's average modem speeds most pages designed for users dialing in from home should contain no more than 50 to 75 kilobytes of graphics.

Graphics and intranets Luckily for graphic designers, many Web sites are created primarily for educational, organizational, and commercial users who access their local intranets and the larger World Wide Web from the school or office at Ethernet speeds or greater. Graphics and page performance are also an issue for these users, but it makes little sense to restrict Web page graphics arbitrarily in the cause of "saving network bandwidth." The bandwidth gearheads always miss the point: graphics are what drew most people to the Web in the first place. If you've got the access speed, indulge!

GRAPHIC FILE FORMATS

Because of the bandwidth issues surrounding networked delivery of information and because image files contain so much information, Web graphics are by necessity compressed. Different graphic file formats employ varying compression schemes, and some are designed to work better than others for certain types of graphics. The two primary Web file formats are GIF and JPEG, but a new and promising image format, PNG, is on the horizon.

GIF FILES

The Graphic Interchange Format was popularized by the CompuServe Information Service in the 1980s as an efficient means to transmit images across data networks. In the early 1990s the original designers of the World Wide Web adopted GIF for its efficiency and widespread familiarity. The overwhelming majority of images on the Web are now in GIF format, and virtually all Web browsers that support graphics can display GIF files. GIF files incorporate a compression scheme to keep file sizes at a minimum, and they are limited to 8-bit (256 or fewer colors) color palettes. Several slight variants of the basic GIF format now add support for a transparent color and for the interlaced GIF graphics popularized by Netscape Navigator.

You may come across references to such different GIF formats as "GIF 87A" and "GIF 89A." All forms of GIF images will work in Web browsers that support the basic GIF format, so you don't have to worry whether your readers will be able to see your GIF graphics no matter which GIF version you use. Users whose browsers support the transparency and interlacing features (such as Netscape Navigator and Microsoft Explorer) will see more sophisticated visual effects, but everyone can see basic GIF images.

GIF *file compression*   The GIF file format uses a relatively basic form of file compression (Lempel Zev Welch, or LZW) that squeezes out inefficiencies in the data storage without losing data or distorting the image. The LZW compression scheme is best at compressing images with large fields of homogeneous color. It is less efficient at compressing complicated pictures with many colors and complex textures:

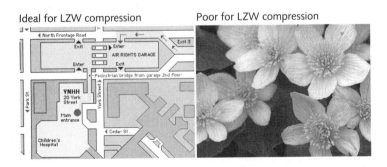

Ideal for LZW compression   Poor for LZW compression

Improving GIF compression   You can take advantage of the characteristics of
LZW compression to improve its efficiency and thereby reduce the size of
your GIF graphics. The strategy is to reduce the number of colors in your GIF
image to the minimum number necessary and to remove stray colors that are
not required to represent the image. A GIF graphic cannot have more than
256 colors but it can have fewer colors, down to the minimum of two (black
and white). Images with fewer colors will compress more efficiently under
LZW compression. When compressing GIF graphics using Photoshop 4.01
(or later) we use the following procedure to convert full-color navigation
and other small page graphics, such as this page footer graphic, to GIF files:

1   Inspect your graphic carefully at high magnification to be sure you have
    removed any unnecessary colors and have simplified the graphic as much
    as possible. Look for and remove random pixels of stray color, and sim-
    plify areas that have more complex shading than is necessary.
2   Make a copy of your full-color original, and perform the following steps
    only on the copy.
3   Change the image mode of the graphic from RGB to "Indexed Color."
    Select the "Web" palette option, and do not dither the image. This forces
    all the colors into browser-safe colors.
4   Switch the image mode back to RGB color.
5   Switch the image mode again to "Indexed Color," but this time choose
    the "Exact" option from the "Color palette" menu. This removes all col-
    ors from the palette except those actually used in the image.
6   "Export" the graphic with the "GIF 89A" export plug-in, and be sure not
    to interlace small graphics.

Interlaced GIF   The conventional (non-interlaced) GIF graphic downloads
one line of pixels at a time from top to bottom, and Web viewers like
Netscape Navigator display each line of the image as it gradually builds on
the screen. In interlaced GIF files the image data is stored in a format that
allows Netscape (and other browsers that support interlaced GIFs) to begin
to build a low-resolution version of the full-sized GIF picture on the screen
while the file is downloading. Many people find the "fuzzy-to-sharp" animated effect of interlacing visually appealing, but the most important benefit of interlacing is that it gives the reader a preview of the full area of the
picture while the picture downloads into the browser.

  Interlacing is best for larger GIF images such as illustrations and photographs. Interlacing is a poor choice for small GIF graphics such as navigation
bars, buttons, and icons. These small graphics will load onto the screen

Half of figure downloaded,
non-interlaced GIF

Half of figure downloaded,
interlaced GIF

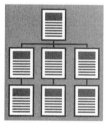

much faster if you keep them in conventional (non-interlaced) GIF format. In general, interlacing has no significant effect on the file size of GIF graphics.

Transparent GIF   The "GIF 89A" format allows you to pick colors from the color lookup table of the GIF to be transparent. You can use image editing software like Photoshop (and many shareware utility programs) to select colors in a GIF graphic's color palette to become transparent. Usually the color selected for transparency is the background color in the graphic.

Plain GIF graphic
with opaque background color

Select the background color
to be transparent

Transparent GIF as it looks
on the page

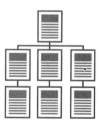

Unfortunately, the transparent property is not selective; if you make a color transparent, every pixel in the graphic that shares that particular color will become also transparent. This can cause unexpected results:

Plain GIF graphic with opaque background color

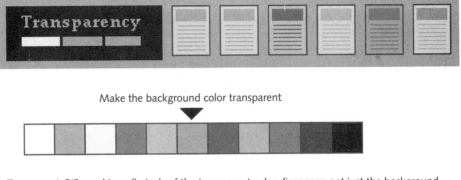

Make the background color transparent

Transparent GIF graphic – all pixels of the transparent color disappear, not just the background

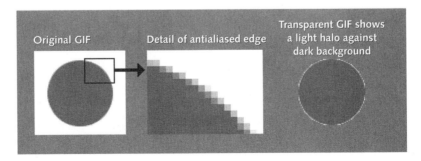

Adding transparency to a GIF graphic can produce disappointing results when the image contains antialiasing (see Chapter 5, *Antialiased type*). If you use an image editing program like Photoshop to create a shape set against a background color, Photoshop will smooth the shape by inserting pixels of intermediate colors along the shape's boundary edges. This smoothing, or antialiasing, improves the look of screen images by softening jagged edges. Trouble starts when you set the background color to transparent and then use the image on a Web page against a different background color. The antialiased pixels in the image will still correspond to the original background color. In the example below, when we change the background color from white to transparent (letting the gray Web page background show through), an ugly white halo appears around the graphic:

Transparency works best with simple diagrammatic graphics, but it can also work with complex shapes. The GIF graphic of the watercolor painting below (from the online version of this guide) can run across the scan column and into the white background because we made the white background of the sparrow painting transparent. We avoided potential problems with a light halo around the leaves in the gray scan column area by retouching the painting to remove the white antialiased "halo" from the leaf edges:

Animated GIF   The GIF file format allows you to combine multiple GIF images into a single file to create an animation. There are a number of drawbacks to this functionality, however. The GIF format applies no compression between frames, so if you are combining four 30-kilobyte images into a single animation, you will end up with a 120 KB GIF file to push through the wire. The other drawback of GIF animations is that they are an imposition and a potential distraction. Because there are no interface controls for this file format, GIF animations play whether you want them to or not. And if looping is enabled, the animations play again and again and again. GIF animations are rarely meaningful and generally distract readers from the main content. If you are using a GIF animation as content – to illustrate a concept or technique – display the animation in a secondary window. That way your readers can view the animation and then close the window. If you present the animation on the main content page, it will interfere with other page elements.

JPEG GRAPHICS
The other graphic file format commonly used on the Web to minimize graphics file sizes is the Joint Photographic Experts Group (JPEG) compression scheme. Unlike GIF graphics, JPEG images are full-color images (24 bit, or "true color"). JPEG images have generated tremendous interest among photographers, artists, graphic designers, medical imaging specialists, art historians, and other groups for whom image quality is paramount and where

color fidelity cannot be compromised by dithering a graphic to 8-bit color. A newer form of JPEG file called "progressive JPEG" gives JPEG graphics the same gradually built display seen in interlaced GIFs. Like interlaced GIFs, progressive JPEG images often take longer to load onto the page than standard JPEGs, but they do offer the reader a quicker preview.

JPEG compression uses a sophisticated mathematical technique called a discrete cosine transformation to produce a sliding scale of graphics compression. You can choose the degree of compression you wish to apply to an image in JPEG format, but in doing so you also determine the image's quality. The more you squeeze a picture with JPEG compression, the more you degrade its quality. JPEG can achieve incredible compression ratios, squeezing graphics down to as much as one hundred times smaller than the original file. This is possible because the JPEG algorithm discards "unnecessary" data as it compresses the image, and it is thus called a "lossy" compression technique. Notice in the example below how increasing the JPEG compression progressively degrades the image:

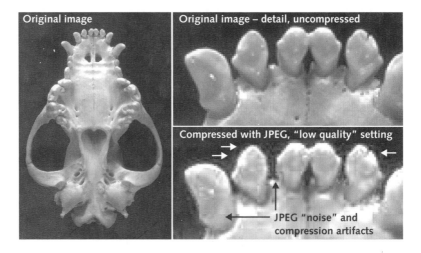

The checkered pattern and the dark "noise" pixels in the compressed image are classic JPEG compression artifacts.

Another example of JPEG compression is shown below. Note the extensive compression noise and distortion present in the bottom dolphin – the download time saved is not worth the degrading of the images.

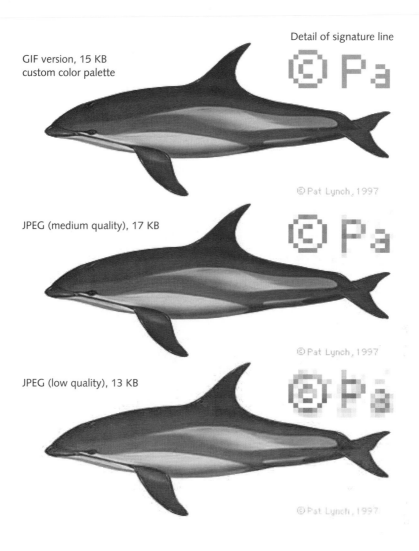

GIF version, 15 KB
custom color palette

Detail of signature line

© Pat Lynch, 1997

JPEG (medium quality), 17 KB

© Pat Lynch, 1997

JPEG (low quality), 13 KB

© Pat Lynch, 1997

Save your original uncompressed images! Once an image is compressed using JPEG compression data is lost and you cannot recover it from that image file. Always save an uncompressed original file of your graphics or photographs as backup.

JPEG image artifacts The JPEG algorithm was optimized for compressing conventional pictorial photographs and is also good at handling complex realistic illustrations that look like photographs. Photos and artwork with smooth color and tonal transitions and with few areas of harsh contrast or sharp edges are ideal for JPEG compression. Yet most page design elements, diagrams, typography within images, and many illustrations are composed of hard-edged graphics and bright color boundaries that are seldom encountered in photographs. The illustration below shows what happens when you compress a diagrammatic image (shown in *a*) in GIF format (*b*, no compression artifacts) and JPEG compression (*c*, with JPEG compression "noise" around the arrowhead and lines):

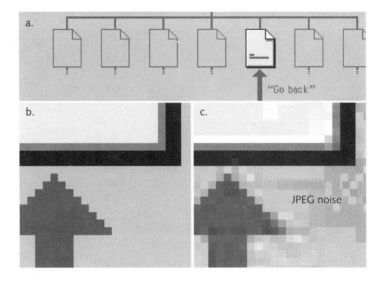

When compressed with JPEG, diagrammatic images show a noise pattern of compression artifacts around the edges of geometric graphics (*c*, above). The JPEG algorithm is best at compressing smooth tonal transitions and cannot properly reproduce the harsh transitions at the edges of diagrammatic graphics.

PNG GRAPHICS

Portable Network Graphic (PNG, pronounced "ping") is a new image format developed by a consortium of graphic software developers as a nonproprietary alternative to the GIF image format. As mentioned earlier, the GIF format was developed by CompuServe, and it uses the proprietary LZW compression scheme owned by Unisys Corporation. Any graphics tool developer who makes software that saves in GIF format must pay a royalty to Unisys and CompuServe.

PNG graphics were designed specifically for use on Web pages, and they offer a range of attractive features that will eventually make PNG the most common graphic format. These features include a full range of color depths, support for sophisticated image transparency, better interlacing, and automatic corrections for display monitor gamma. PNG images can also hold a short text description of the image's content. You will be able to use Internet search engines to search for images based on these embedded text descriptions. Unfortunately, the PNG graphic format is not yet widely supported, and the current implementation of PNG graphics in Netscape Navigator and

Microsoft Internet Explorer does not fully support all of PNG's features. This will change over the next few years, but do not make a commitment to PNG graphics until you are sure that most of your audience is using browsers that support PNG.

IMAGING STRATEGIES

Interface elements   Small page navigation graphics, buttons, and graphic design elements should always be handled as non-interlaced GIF graphics that use the standard 216-color browser palette so that they never dither, even on 8-bit display screens.

Photographs as GIFs   When you convert a full-color image into an 8-bit (256-color) GIF file you could allow Photoshop to choose the 256 colors that best fit that particular image. This results in the optimal GIF image quality – often these images look almost as good as their full-color originals – but the creation of a custom color palette does have drawbacks. If the reader of your page has a monitor that shows only 256 colors at one time (like most older Windows and Macintosh color displays), then the colors in your GIF images will appear distorted as the browser forces them to display using the 216-color browser palette. Forcing a GIF made from custom palette colors to display within the limited system palette colors can result in ugly distortions of the image. A Web browser running on an 8-bit display has no way to optimize your particular custom GIF colors – it forces the picture to display in the nearest equivalent colors in the browser palette. The result is often color banding, or harsh distortions of the original colors, as seen in the example below:

GIF file with custom color palette
(256 colors)

GIF file with Web-safe color palette
(216 colors)

To get around this problem you can convert all your color graphics to GIF files that use only the browser palette of 216 colors. This will ensure that your images look exactly the same no matter how the user's display screen is set up. Or you could apply custom palettes to your images and accept that those readers using 8-bit display monitors will see distorted images. Or you could use the JPEG file format instead.

Photographs as JPEGs   JPEG files are inherently full-color (24-bit) images, so preserving the correct colors in the files themselves is not an issue. However, there is no way to prevent JPEG images from dithering when they are displayed on 8-bit screens – any photographic image displayed on a 256-color display will dither. The dithering seen in JPEG images does not compromise image quality any more than if you dithered the images to 256-color GIFs yourself. If you standardize on JPEG images, at least some of your audience will see full-color photographs and illustrations, and the number of readers who have full-color displays grows every day. It is more practical to standardize on the JPEG format for most photographic Web site content because it offers both a reasonable compromise for current display technology and the promise of longer-term utility as full-color display monitors become the norm in personal computing.

Diagrams and illustrations as vector graphics   Most Web page graphics are raster images – often called "bitmap" or "paint" images – composed of a grid of colored pixels. Complex diagrams or illustrations, however, should be created as vector graphics and then converted to raster formats like GIF or JPEG for the Web. Vector graphics (also known as "draw" or "PostScript" graphics) are composed of mathematical descriptions of lines and shapes. Although these graphics cannot be used directly to illustrate Web pages without requiring users to have a special browser plug-in, there are three major reasons for producing complex diagrams in vector graphics programs:

1 Vector graphic illustrations are automatically antialiased when imported into Photoshop or other raster imaging programs and converted to raster graphics:

Illustrator artwork, imported
but not antialiased

Same graphic, antialiased on
import into Photoshop

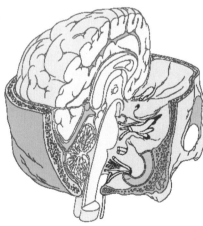
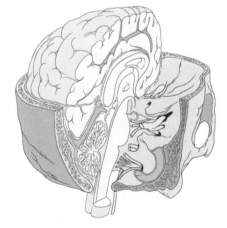

2 Vector graphics can be easily resized as they are imported:

Three Photoshop renderings from
the same PostScript vector
drawing, antialiased

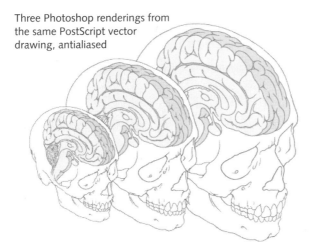

3 Complex artwork created in such vector-based programs as Adobe
Illustrator and Macromedia FreeHand is a better investment of your illustration budget, because vector graphics also produce high-resolution
images suitable for print, as shown below. The illustrations below and immediately above were produced from the same Illustrator file:

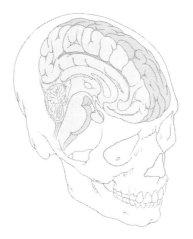

Archiving your Web site graphics Always save a copy of your original graphics files, and make it a standard practice to create separate new files every
time you make significant changes to an image, such as resizing it or changing the file format. After the close of a project all photos and artwork should
be kept and stored at their full original resolution and in a format that does
not compromise the image quality of the files through "lossy" image compression, as in JPEG. We prefer to archive every image generated in a proj-

ect. Many small 8-bit GIF or JPEG illustrations on the finished Web page, for example, start out as much larger high-resolution files in Photoshop format. We save all the intermediate pieces, not just the original and final files. This will save you a lot of time if you later change your mind about the best file format for a graphic or need to modify it. If you have archived the full-color Photoshop version of the graphic, you can easily create a new version in a different format. If you save only the final GIFs, you will have lost your full-color version. If you save only the final JPEGs, you will no longer have images without compression artifacts, and recompressing an image that already has JPEG compression noise usually yields poor results.

SUMMARY-FILE FORMATS

Uses for GIF and JPEG files Netscape Navigator, Microsoft Internet Explorer, and most other browsers support both GIF and JPEG graphics (as of this writing, PNG graphics are not adequately supported). In theory, you could use either graphic format for the visual elements of your Web pages. In practice, however, most Web developers will continue to favor the GIF format for most page design elements, diagrams, and images that must not dither on 8-bit display screens. Designers choose the JPEG format mostly for photographs, complex "photographic" illustrations, medical images, and other types of images in which the compression artifacts of the JPEG process do not severely compromise image quality.

Advantages of GIF Files
- GIF is the most widely supported graphics format on the Web
- You can make images that will not dither on 8-bit displays
- GIFs of diagrammatic images look better than JPEGs
- GIF supports transparency and interlacing

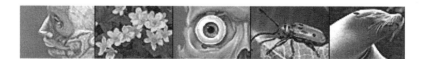

Advantages of JPEG images
- Huge compression ratios mean faster download speeds
- JPEG produces excellent results for most photographs and medical images
- JPEG supports full-color (24-bit, "true color") images

IMAGES ON THE SCREEN

The primary challenge in creating images for Web pages is the relatively low resolution of the computer screen. But today's computer screens can display thousands or millions of colors, and this wealth of color minimizes the limitations of screen resolution. Complex graphics or color photographs often look surprisingly good on Web pages for two reasons:

- True-color (24-bit) or high-color (16-bit) displays show enough colors to reproduce photographs and complex art accurately
- The light transmitted from display monitors shows more dynamic range and color intensity than light reflected from printed pages

Science and education users are now realizing that digital publishing is color publishing – on the Web there is no economic penalty for publishing in color. Web pages may in fact be the best current means of distributing color photography – it's a lot cheaper than color printing, and it's also more consistent and reliable than all but the most expert (and costly) color printing.

THE SCREEN VERSUS PRINTED COLOR ARTWORK

Relative to printed pages the computer screen is a low-resolution medium. When you look at illustrations, photographs, and other sophisticated imagery, however, the differences in quality between conventional four-color printing and the computer screen are not as great as you might expect.

In terms of resolution, the computer screen is limited to about 72 to 92 dots per inch of resolution (see *Screen resolution*, above). But most four-color magazine printing is done at 150 dpi, or only about four times the resolution of the computer screen (150 dpi is four times the resolution of 75 dpi because resolution is measured over area, 150 × 150 per square inch):

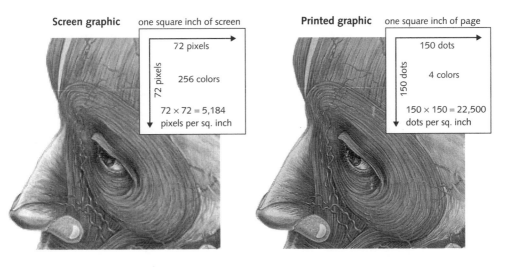

Screen graphic one square inch of screen

72 pixels

72 pixels

256 colors

72 × 72 = 5,184 pixels per sq. inch

Printed graphic one square inch of page

150 dots

150 dots

4 colors

150 × 150 = 22,500 dots per sq. inch

Regarding color reproduction, four-color printed images are separated into four subtractive printing colors (cyan, magenta, yellow, and black). These four inks combined produce the illusion of a full range of colors on the printed page, but ultimately the typical magazine or textbook image is composed of only four colors. By comparison, as mentioned, current computer monitors can display a minimum of 256 colors, producing a richness of color that easily rivals the best color printing. Also, computer screens display transilluminated images – the colored light shines out from the screen. Transilluminated images deliver a much greater range of contrast and color intensity than images printed on opaque paper, which depend on reflected light. Finally, computer displays show color images using the additive RGB (red-green-blue) color system, which can display a much broader and subtler range of colors than conventional four-color printing.

Bottom line: the computer screen is lower in resolution, but because of the other advantages of computer displays, images on Web pages can easily rival color images printed on paper.

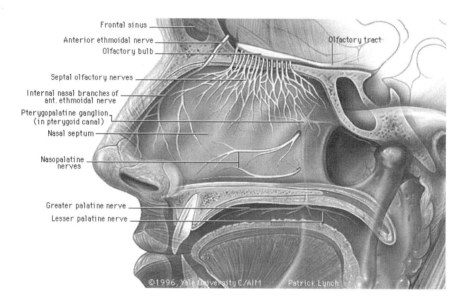

COMPLEX ILLUSTRATIONS OR PHOTOGRAPHS

The anatomic graphic above was originally painted at much higher resolution in Adobe Photoshop (1000 × 2000 pixels, 24-bit RGB file). We then reduced a copy to the size above and used Photoshop's "Unsharp Mask" filter (at 60 percent) to restore sharpness. Although this small version of the painting has lost some resolution and color detail, it still shows all the major anatomic landmarks. The extra detail and subtle nuances of high-resolution artwork are not entirely lost when the graphic is reduced to Web page size.

We chose the JPEG file format for the anatomic painting because the art-work is relatively large for a Web page graphic. JPEG compression can be used for paintings or photographs with text labels if you choose the right compression setting. The painting above was compressed in Photoshop at "good" quality, which is the medium-quality setting ("excellent, good, poor"). If you choose the "good" or "excellent" JPEG compression settings, text labels should look acceptable, at least on 16-bit or 24-bit displays. Note that in the anatomic illustration example shown above the text labels are clear and legible, even though close inspection would certainly turn up JPEG noise around the characters.

DIAGRAMS FOR THE COMPUTER SCREEN

Basic diagrams also work well on the computer screen if they are carefully designed to match the grid of pixels on the screen. Graphics built with or-thogonal lines (straight horizontal or vertical lines) or diagonal lines at 45-degree angles work best for the screen, as this enlarged view illustrates:

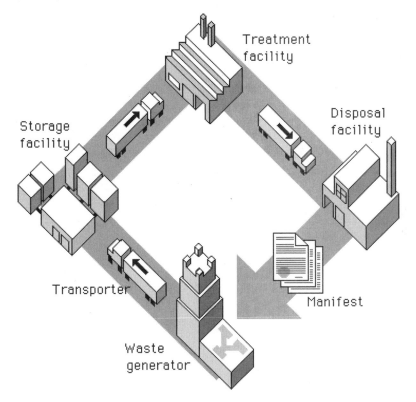

Complex icons are hard to interpret, and they look mushy and confusing on the screen. Keep icons and navigation graphics as simple as possible:

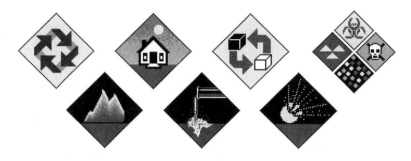

Simple isometric perspective graphics also work well because they depend on straight lines and 45-degree diagonals. Although the restrictions of working within fixed line angles make the technique unsuitable for many diagrammatic graphics, it is possible to build complex illustrations using this technique. The regularity of the isometric line work and the absence of the complexities of perspective bring order to graphics that might otherwise be too complex for Web page presentation:

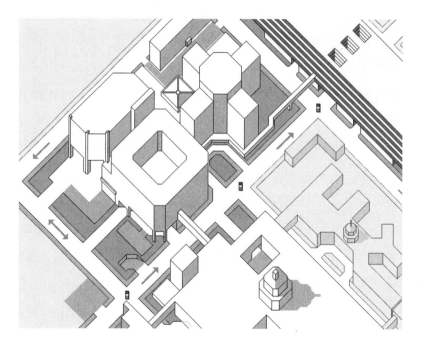

Another benefit of keeping diagrammatic art and maps simple is that graphic simplicity is ideally suited to the LZW encoding compression algorithm used in GIF graphics (see GIF *files*, above). This 828 × 525-pixel GIF graphic is large for a Web page, but it compresses to a mere 27 KB because the contents are well suited to LZW compression:

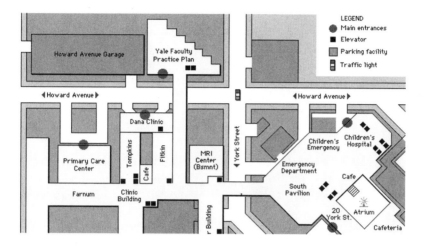

Be careful about choosing the proper sizes for this type of illustration. Graphics carefully built to match the pixel grid cannot be resized automatically in Photoshop – they must be redrawn by hand to larger or smaller sizes to avoid a mushy, fuzzy look that destroys their effectiveness:

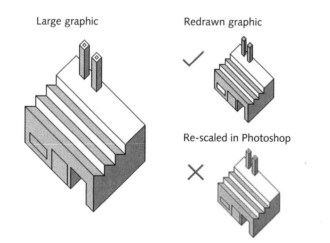

The low resolution of the computer screen is insufficient for displaying diagrams that incorporate many curves or angles; lines that do not follow the pixel grid appear jagged. To optimize these kinds of diagrams for Web pages you'll need to use antialiasing to smooth the boundaries and make the jagged edges less apparent:

Not antialiased   Antialiased

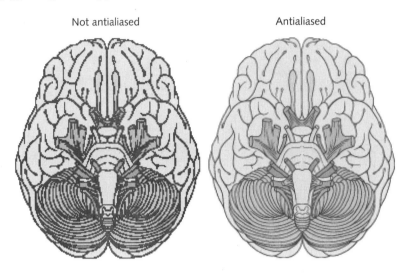

At great magnification antialiased graphics may have fuzzy boundaries, but at normal magnification antialiasing produces smooth, natural-looking line work.

HTML AND GRAPHICS

Height and width tags   All your page graphics source tags (even small button or icon graphics) should include HEIGHT and WIDTH tags. These tags tell the browser how much space to devote to a graphic on a page, and they instruct the browser to lay out your Web page even before the graphics files have begun to download. Although this does not speed up downloading (only a faster data connection can do that), it does allow the user to see the page layout more quickly. The text blocks will fill out first and then the graphics files will "pour" into the allotted spaces. This means that the user can start to read your page while the graphics are downloading.

HEIGHT and WIDTH tags are additions to the basic image source tag:

```
<IMG SRC="picture.gif" HEIGHT="150" WIDTH="535">
```

Colored backgrounds   Web background colors offer a "zero-bandwidth" means to change the look of your pages without adding graphics. They also allow you to increase the legibility of your pages, tune the background color to complement foreground art, and signal a broad change in context from one part of your site to another. *HotWired* magazine has long used bold background colors as an easy way of enlivening the visual impact of their otherwise low-bandwidth pages:

Picking the background color is easy in WYSIWYG (what you see is what you get) graphic Web page layout programs. Unfortunately, picking a color without one of these Web page editors is a procedure only a propellerhead could enjoy. The color is specified in the tag in hexadecimal code, in which the six elements give the red, green, and blue values that blend to make the color. In the tag, the hex code is always preceded by a "#" sign: (#RRGGBB). Because this whole business is handled visually by the new generation of WYSIWYG page editors, we will not delve further into the arcana of hexadecimal RGB color selection.

Using the HTML extensions for changing the color of page backgrounds, text, and link colors is easy – you simply add a few extensions to the BODY tag at the beginning of your HTML code for the page (this particular tag yields a white background):

```
<BODY BGCOLOR="#FFFFFF">
```

Background colors and legibility   Shifting the page background from gray to white is really the only alteration of the standard Web page background that we can recommend if your highest priority is screen legibility. The legibility of type on the computer screen is already compromised by the low resolution of the computer screen. The typical Macintosh or Windows computer screen displays text at 72 to 80 dots per inch (about 5,200 dots per square inch), or almost 300 times lower resolution than a typical magazine page (1,440,000 dots per square inch). Black text on a white (or very light gray) background yields the best overall type contrast and legibility. Black backgrounds are significantly less legible than white backgrounds, even when white type is used for maximum contrast. Colored backgrounds can work as an alternative to plain browser-default gray if the colors are kept in very muted tones, and low in overall color saturation (pastels, light grays, and light earth tones work best).

Background patterns   Early in 1995 Netscape Navigator version 1.1 gave Web page authors the ability to use small tiled GIF or JPEG graphics (or a single large graphic) to form a background pattern behind the Web page. The feature is controversial in Web design discussions, because pages that use large background images take much longer to download and because the background patterns tend to make pages harder to read unless they are carefully designed.

To be suitable for use as a background texture, the graphic should be a small GIF or JPEG, ideally no more than about 100 × 100 pixels in size. In our experience, JPEG background patterns load slightly faster than equivalent GIF graphics. Typical graphics used for background patterns are homogeneous textures:

Background graphics are added to a Web page by modifying the BODY HTML tag:

```
<BODY BACKGROUND="example.jpg">
```

When your browser sees the BACKGROUND tag, it will tile the graphic file "example.jpg" across the page, under the text and any other graphics. Older Web browsers that do not support background images will ignore the BACKGROUND tag and assign a default white or gray background.

How you might use background textures depends entirely on your goals for your Web site, the access speeds that are typical for your target audience, and whether the multimedia/CD-ROM-style look (fast becoming a cliché) meets the aesthetic goals of your Web site. Using large or visually complex background textures on any page that is heavily accessed by busy people looking for work-related information is foolish – the long download times, unprofessional aesthetics, and poor legibility will annoy your users. That said, in the hands of skilled graphic designers creating Web pages specifically designed for graphic impact, the option to use background textures opens up many interesting visual design possibilities. This is particularly true in universities and commercial organizations where fast network access is commonplace and bandwidth is not the obstacle it is with modem-based users. Our advice is to stay away from complex background images or textures – the chances of making a bad functional and aesthetic mistake are high.

IMAGEMAPS

Imagemaps offer a way to define multiple "live" link areas within a graphic on a Web page. For example, you can make a banner graphic for the top of your page and embed multiple "button" areas within it. The header and footer graphics used in our Web style guide are simple imagemaps. This is how the header graphic would look if you could see the "live" areas defined in the imagemap:

graphics.html

background.html

Yale C/AIM Web Style Guide

Server-side imagemaps versus client-side imagemaps   Web imagemaps used to have a reputation for being complex to implement and slow to execute because the original procedure for creating imagemaps on Web pages required reference to a separate file on the host Web server each time a user clicked on an imagemap. This "server-side" imagemap technology was needlessly complex and very inefficient. Since early 1996 the major Web browsers have supported "client-side" imagemaps, in which the information on what areas of a graphic are "live" links is incorporated within the HTML code for the Web page. Most Web page layout programs now incorporate easy graphic interfaces for setting up imagemaps, so we do not discuss the HTML technical details here. (See the reference links in the companion Web site.)

Space-efficient graphic impact   Imagemaps have become a standard feature of most professionally designed Web sites because they offer an effective combination of visual appeal and, when used properly, space-efficient functionality. Imagemaps are particularly effective when incorporated into moderately sized "splash" graphics at the top of home pages or into the "signature" graphics or logos that define your pages. For example, Sun Microsystems uses a space-efficient imagemap menu on its home page as a scan column along the left edge of the page. The graphic is not just a menu; it helps define the signature "look" of pages within the Sun Web site:

Graphic flexibility   Imagemaps are the only means to incorporate multiple links into a graphic illustration, as in this anatomic example:

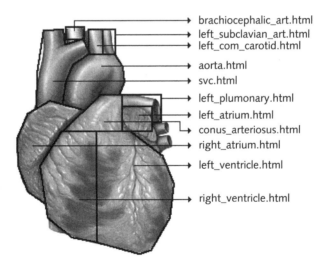

Imagemaps are also the ultimate way to overcome the vertical, list-oriented, graphically inflexible norms of conventional Web pages built with standard HTML tags. With imagemaps you can abandon HTML page layout and build links into large graphics, just as you might in CD-ROM authoring programs. Keep in mind, however, that such designs are suitable only for audiences with high bandwidth access to the Web or the local intranet.

8 *Multimedia*

For time is the medium of narration, as it is the medium of life.
– Thomas Mann, *The Magic Mountain*

PERHAPS THE MOST POWERFUL aspect of computing technology is the ability to combine text, graphics, sounds, and moving images in meaningful ways. The promise of multimedia has been slow to reach the Web because of bandwidth limitations, but each day brings new solutions. Although there are numerous methods for creating Web multimedia, we recommend using stable technology that works for the great majority of client machines. Plug-ins that extend the capabilities of your Web pages are a mixed blessing. You risk losing your audience if you require them to jump through hoops to view your content.

APPLICATIONS FOR MULTIMEDIA

Web designers must always be considerate of the consumer. A happy customer will come back, but one who has been made to wait and is then offered goods that are irrelevant is likely to shop elsewhere. Because multimedia comes with a high price tag, it should be used sparingly and judiciously.

Splash screens, or site covers, are a common location for multimedia elements. Like this book's cover, splash screens are intended to entice users into a site – to open the book and read what's inside. Animations and sound can pique a user's curiosity, leading them into the site. We do not recommend using multimedia elements for "splash" in the interior of a site. Any page element that is not relevant to the content is simply distracting, particularly one that talks or winks or twirls.

Animation frames

Multimedia as content enhances many Web presentations. A site about poetry might include recitations, a text about a composer could include excerpts from his or her work, a language site might include pronunciations. Animations could be used to present simulations and video to support historical content. There are technical limitations to the delivery of audiovisual content via the Web, however. Long-duration video and video requiring smooth motion or clear details require large amounts of bandwidth to deliver and may tax the playback capacity of the client machine. A significant amount of downsampling and compression is required to create a file that is small enough to be delivered via the Web. In some cases, these compromises may be too significant to warrant the effort. When you are considering adding multimedia to your pages, make sure the technology can meet the demands of your content. You do not want users to expend extra time and energy to retrieve files that cannot be illustrative owing to limitations of the technology.

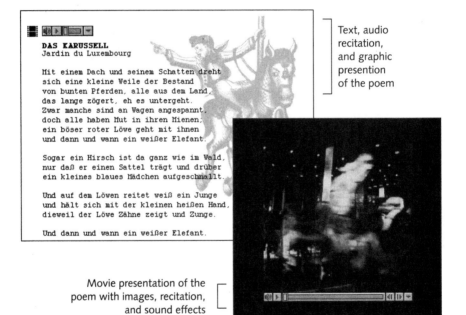

Text, audio recitation, and graphic presention of the poem

Movie presentation of the poem with images, recitation, and sound effects

Plug-ins that allow users to see new and exciting things using their favorite browser software are constantly being introduced. This is especially true of multimedia; the options for encoding and delivering audio, animations, and video are dizzying. Although designers may be tempted to create files that employ the functionality offered by custom plug-ins, they should bear two things in mind. First, the bother and potential confusion of downloading and installing plug-ins will deter many users. Second, it is not prudent to create content in a custom file format that could quickly become obsolete. It is best to create your multimedia content in the standard formats for operating systems and browser software.

This somewhat conservative discussion of multimedia considerations needs one important qualification. If you are creating a site for a specific audience and not for global interests you will probably have more flexibility and can ask more from your users. You can require them to use specific browser software and plug-ins, and you can include data-intensive multimedia elements in your presentation. Say, for example, that your site is academic and your audience is a group of students or faculty with specialized interests. You are charged with the task of creating a custom site that fully addresses these interests, so function should define form. A site on German poetry for a German literature class could contain bandwidth-intensive audio and video elements because the students who access the site will use these multimedia elements to enhance their understanding of the poetry. These students are not casual visitors; they are invested in the content, so they will tolerate lengthy download times and more demanding site interaction. And because your audience is defined and finite, you can take steps to ensure that they know what to expect and are prepared when they visit your site.

DESIGN AND MULTIMEDIA ELEMENTS

The combination of low bandwidth considerations and primitive interface options creates interesting design challenges for Web developers who wish to incorporate multimedia elements into their sites. Designers should both inform users when they are entering a high bandwidth area and give them the tools they need to control their experience once in the area.

Visitors to your site need to be informed about high bandwidth areas before entering them. Explain clearly on the contents page of your site where you are sending users so that they know what's in store for them before they decide to go there. Also explain what browser software and plug-ins are required so that users will not be confronted with unfriendly dialog boxes. Most casual visitors will not stay if they have to download custom software; it's too easy to go elsewhere.

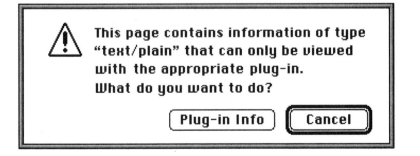

As with all data-intensive site elements, be certain that your multimedia content is relevant. If someone has come to your site to learn more about Web style guidelines and you show them a video of your pet hamster, you will certainly annoy your visitors and you could lose your audience.

Be sure to give users status information and controls when you are presenting multimedia materials. The QuickTime controller bar is an extremely effective interface element that provides both controls and status information. It allows users both to adjust the volume control and to play, stop, and scrub through a movie, and it provides information about the movie's download status.

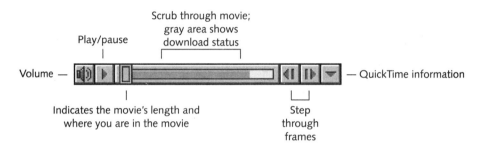

If you don't include controls, users will hit your page with no way to control their viewing environment. If, for example, a visitor is looking at your page at a public workstation and you have looping bird calls as a background sound without any control options, the visitor will experience an unsettling (and potentially embarrassing) moment when he or she cannot control interaction with your site.

WEB MULTIMEDIA STRATEGIES

Simply because we *can* digitize hours worth of analog video and stream it out over the Web doesn't mean that we *should*. The value of having the text of *Paradise Lost* on computer is not in making it available for reading – most people prefer to read the work in print. We digitize texts in order to use the strengths of computing, such as searching and linking, to enhance our understanding of the material. This holds true for multimedia, too: we need to consider how best to use the computer and not simply translate analog video and audio content to the computer screen. Networked multimedia requires scaling and compression, which means that much of the content created for analog delivery does not work well on the Web. The key to successful Web multimedia is to tailor your content for Web delivery.

AUDIO ONLY
Audio is an extremely efficient way to deliver information. Consider a training video on measuring and weighing chemical compounds. Which track –

audio or video – would be the most important in conveying information? In the sound track a narrator explains the procedure, and in the video track someone is measuring and weighing compounds. Which track would you remove if necessary? Which could stand on its own? The audio track. Consider enhancing your presentation with an audio component. Audio can be captured and optimized fairly easily, and it compresses well.

When recording original audio, take the time to do it right. Low-frequency background noises, such as the hum of a ventilation system, will be inseparable from your audio track; no amount of tweaking will eliminate it altogether. Remember, too, that the downsampling and compression you will have to perform to make your audio Web deliverable will emphasize any flaws in your recording.

SLIDE SHOWS

Slide shows are another method for delivering multimedia on the Web. In a slide show, you synchronize audio with still images. Through this approach you provide information via audio and add visual emphasis with still images. As an example, to present the training video mentioned above as a slide show, you would use video editing software to synchronize the narration with still images of the weighing and measuring procedure. Still images compress much more efficiently than video, and because slide shows do not require smooth motion, the movie frame rate can be low. This in turn means that you can devote more data to image quality and size.

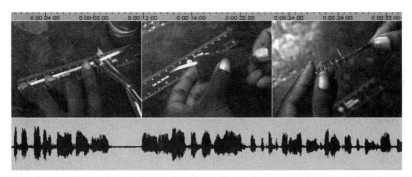

Use video editing software to synchronize audio and images and create a slide show.

VIDEO

Video is the most challenging multimedia content to deliver via the Web. One second of uncompressed NTSC (National Television Standards Committee) video, the international standard for television and video, requires approximately 27 megabytes of disk storage space. The amount of scaling and compression required to turn this quantity of data into something that can be used on a network is significant, sometimes so much so as to render the material useless. If at all possible, tailor your video content for the Web.

- Shoot original video; that way you can take steps to create video that will compress efficiently and still look good at low resolution and frame rates.
- Shoot close-ups. Wide shots have too much detail to make sense at low resolution.

Wide shot, too much detail   Close shots work better at low resolution

- Shoot against a simple monochromatic background whenever possible. This will make small video images easier to understand and will increase the efficiency of compression.
- Use a tripod to minimize camera movement. A camera locked in one position will minimize the differences between frames and greatly improve video compression.
- Avoid zooming and panning. These can make low frame-rate movies confusing to view and interpret and can cause them to compress poorly.
- When editing your video, use hard cuts between shots. Don't use the transitional effects offered by video editing software, such as dissolves or elaborate wipes, because they will not compress efficiently and will not play smoothly on the Web.
- If you are digitizing material that was originally recorded for video or film, choose your material carefully. Look for clips that contain minimal motion and lack essential but small details. Motion and detail are the most obvious shortcomings of low-resolution video.

ANIMATION

Most Web animation requires special plug-ins for viewing. The exception is the animated GIF format, which is by far the most prevalent animation format on the Web. The animation option of the GIF format combines individual GIF images into a single file to create an animation. You can set the animation to loop on the page or to play once, and you can designate the duration for each frame in the animation.

Using animated GIFs has several drawbacks. One concerns the user interface. GIF animations do not provide interface controls, so users have no easy way to stop a looping animation or to replay a nonlooping animation. Second, animations generally are nothing more than a distraction. An animation that appears alongside primary content will simply disrupt your readers' concentration and keep them from the objective of your site. Finally, the animated GIF format does not perform interframe compression, which means that if you create a ten-frame animation and each frame is a 20 KB GIF, you'll be putting a 200 KB file on your page.

There is a place for animations on the Web, however. A simple animation on a Web site's cover, or "splash" screen, can provide just the right amount of mystery to invite users to explore your materials. The essential content on a site cover is typically a menu of links, so the threat of distraction is less than it would be on an internal content page. Animations can also be useful in illustrating simple concepts or procedures. One way to present animations as content is to show them in a secondary window using the TARGET="main" parameter of the A HREF HTML tag. This technique offers a measure of viewer control; readers can open the window to view the animation and then close the window when they're through.

MULTIMEDIA PROCESSING

AUDIO PROCESSING
Normalize   Audio files may lose amplitude and clarity in the digitizing process. To compensate you can use sound editing software to normalize your audio. This process finds the highest peak in a file and then amplifies the entire file to make that peak's volume 100 percent. This ensures that you are working with the loudest possible audio signal.

Boost the midrange   Another way to enhance your Web audio is to use the software's equalizer function to boost slightly the midrange frequencies.

VIDEO PROCESSING
Process the audio   Extract the audio track from your video and perform the audio normalizing and equalizing mentioned above, then synchronize the processed audio with the video track.

Trim clips   Make sure that your movie begins and ends with frames that make sense as still images. The first frame will appear on the user's screen while the movie is loading, and the last frame will remain on screen when the movie has finished. Take care that these images do not seem awkward out of the context of the movie.

Crop   Use video editing software to remove unwanted noise or borders from the movie image. Cropping trims rows of pixels from the edges of a clip and then resizes the clip to its original dimensions.

Scale   Most Web video is sized to quarter-screen (320×240 pixels) or smaller.

COMPRESSION

Analog source generally comes with certain established characteristics. CD-quality audio source is sampled at 44.1 kHz, 16-bit stereo sound. Video source is usually 640 × 480 pixels in dimension and at a rate of 30 frames per second (fps). Analog source digitized at full resolution requires enormous amounts of disk storage and is far to large to be used on a network. One way to prepare media for network delivery is to reduce the data by, for example, downsampling the audio material to 11.025 kHz, 8-bit mono sound. This reduces the file's size, but it also substantially reduces its quality. Another way to reduce file size is to apply compression.

Compression first eliminates redundant data from a file and then removes less important data to shrink file size still further. This process is achieved using algorithms, or "codecs" (short for compressors/decompressors), that handle the compression of media and the decompression when it is played. Codecs compress files by examining consecutive frames and storing the differences (temporal compression) and/or by generalizing an image and removing redundant data (spatial compression). The process of analyzing each frame and compressing a movie can take a long time, but decompression takes place in real time for smooth playback.

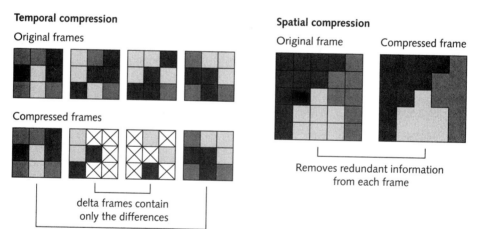

Temporal compression

Original frames

Compressed frames

delta frames contain
only the differences

keyframes contain the entire image

Spatial compression

Original frame   Compressed frame

Removes redundant information
from each frame

The codecs that are used for Web delivery use lossy compression: the process removes data from the original source material. You should never compress material multiple times, because each process will lower the video quality.

In compressing for Web delivery, you should aim to achieve a data rate that can be accommodated by the average network connection and desktop machine of your target audience. The data rate, normally measured in kilobytes per second (KBPS), is the amount of data that is used to represent one second of movie playback. For users to play your files in real time, you need to set a data transmission rate that is slightly lower than the throughput of your users' connections. For a 28.8 modem this means a data rate of approximately 2 KBps, for ISDN lines about 5 KBps, and for T-1 lines (dedicated phone connections) from 5 to 40 KBps. For intranet connections the data rate should be the amount that can be accommodated by the local network being used for delivery.

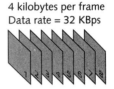

32 KBps received = real-time playback

8 frames per second
4 kilobytes per frame
Data rate = 32 KBps

32 KBps network capacity

For users to view media content in real time, the movie data rate must be less than or equal to the throughput capacity of their connection

The parameters that influence the data rate for audio are:
- Frequency: reducing the frequency reduces the data required to represent the material.
- Depth: 16-bit samples provide greater dynamic range but take up more space. Reducing the depth to 8-bit will reduce the file size (although some audio compression works only with 16-bit samples).
- Channels: be sure not to use stereo settings for a mono source. If your source does have stereo audio, you might consider switching to mono to reduce the data rate.
- Codec: applying compression to an audio track may allow you to keep higher-quality audio settings.

The parameters that influence the data rate for video are:
- Image size: most Web video is scaled to quarter-screen (320 × 240 pixels) or smaller.
- Image quality: reducing the image-quality setting of a movie reduces the data that is stored for each frame.
- Frame rate: standard NTSC video has a frame rate of 30 fps. Most Web video is set to about 10 fps.
- Codec: some codecs compress more efficiently than others, though usually at the expense of image quality (see *Video codecs,* below).
- Custom filters: compression software provides filters that reduce the differences between frames, permitting more efficient compression.
- Audio: the audio track of video can be downsampled and/or compressed to reduce the overall movie data rate.

MULTIMEDIA DELIVERY

The technology of networked media consists of three main components: the server, the network, and the client machine. These three components must work in tandem to deliver good Web multimedia to the desktop. It makes no difference how high-end your video server and network are if your users are running low-end desktop machines that cannot handle the demands of playback.

The wildest of all these wild cards is bandwidth. If you purchase a high-end media server, you can expect a certain level of performance. You can predict playback performance on desktop machines. These elements are somewhat measurable. But unless you are working with a dedicated network, bandwidth will be hugely variable and difficult to predict. Issues regarding bandwidth run from the basic configuration of your connection to the network to the amount of network traffic at any given time.

Given these variables, the parameters for creating and delivering Web multimedia are not easily defined. They will vary depending on the scope and content of your project. If you are creating a Web site for a corporate intranet, for example, your media can be more technologically demanding than if you send it worldwide over the Internet. The key is to be well acquainted with the configuration of your client base and prepare accordingly.

STREAMING

Streaming technology sends data to the desktop continuously but does not download the entire file. In the optimal scenario, the content is stored on a media server, which maintains a constant conversation with the client to determine how much data the user can support. Based on this information, the server adjusts the data stream accordingly and sends just enough data to the client.

Web page with streaming media

1 Browser requests playback via streaming media player
2 Server begins sending media packets
3 Player buffers small amount of incoming stream, then begins playback. Downloading and buffering continue during playback. Media plays directly from buffer to display and then is discarded. Playback will be interrupted if the buffer empties or the network drops packets.

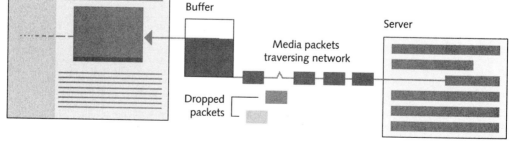

Buffer

Server

Media packets
traversing network

Dropped
packets

Streaming offers many benefits, the first of which is random access. Streaming technology permits movies to be viewed at any point in the video stream. If your reader is accessing an hour's worth of video and wishes to view only the last five minutes, he or she can use the controls to move forward to the desired starting point. Another benefit is low storage demands on the client machine. Streaming media plays directly to the display; it is not stored in memory or on the hard drive.

The strengths of streaming are also its shortcomings. To play a movie in real time the player software needs to keep up with the incoming data sent from the server. As a result, if there are glitches in the network or if the client machine cannot handle playback, the data may simply be lost. Streaming playback requires significant processing power, so playback may be suboptimal if the processor has to drop frames to keep up with the incoming stream. Also, streaming media needs to be heavily compressed to create a file small enough to play in real time.

DOWNLOADING

Downloadable media is temporarily stored on the client machine, in memory or on the hard drive. Most downloadable media is progressive, which means that the information necessary for playback is stored at the beginning of the file. Progressive download allows playback before the entire file has downloaded. Downloadable media is sent to the client using the same HTTP protocol as a Web page, so no special server is required. As long as the download speed stays above the data rate of the movie, playback will be uninterrupted.

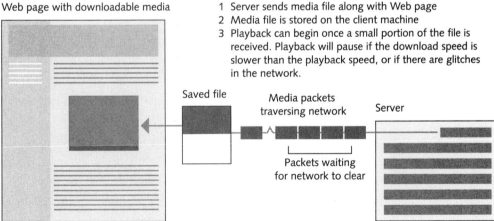

Web page with downloadable media

1 Server sends media file along with Web page
2 Media file is stored on the client machine
3 Playback can begin once a small portion of the file is received. Playback will pause if the download speed is slower than the playback speed, or if there are glitches in the network.

Saved file

Media packets traversing network

Server

Packets waiting for network to clear

The quality of downloadable media is generally higher than that of streaming media. Because the data rate is not required to remain low enough to play the material in real time, more data can be devoted to image quality and motion. Downloadable media also has integrity. All the data in the original movie is contained in the downloaded version. This means that playback is predictable and that you can download the data onto your disk for future use.

The main drawback of downloadable media is the storage demand it places on the client machine. Even videos of short duration require many megabytes of storage. The other problem is that downloadable media does not allow random access. If you want to view only the last few minutes of a long clip you must wait for the entire clip to download. One solution to both of these problems is to split longer media segments into smaller chunks. This reduces the demands on the client machine and allows users more direct access to the material they want.

RECOMMENDATIONS

The technology we recommend for most audio and video content is Apple's QuickTime. QuickTime is cross-platform and has the largest installed user base of any digital audiovisual format. The QuickTime plug-in is part of most browser software, so most users will be able to access your multimedia content without having to install special software. The architecture of QuickTime currently is progressive download, or "fast-start," which allows users to start playing audio and video before the entire file has downloaded. Future versions of QuickTime will employ streaming technology, which will allow random access and eliminate the storage demands of downloadable media.

VIDEO CODECS

SORENSON

The Sorenson Video Codec is the first high-quality, low-bandwidth video codec provided with QuickTime. It is the codec of choice for Web video. Sorenson video plays back smoothly on low- and high-end machines.

CINEPAK

Cinepak is the standard codec for CD-ROM video. Cinepak is often used for Web video even though it was not devised for low-bandwidth video. It takes a long time to compress a movie using Cinepak, but decompression takes place in real-time and Cinepak movies play smoothly on most machines. The image quality produced by Cinepak is patchy and pixelated, particularly in segments that contain detail or motion.

The Photo-JPEG codec produces movies with excellent image quality but they require significant amounts of processing power for playback. This is especially true for large image and/or high frame-rate movies. This codec is well suited for slide shows that use low frame rates and do not contain special video transitions such as dissolves or wipes.

MPEG

MPEG (short for Moving Picture Experts Group, its developer) is a format and a codec at the same time – it is a file format that employs compression algorithms. MPEG video places great demands on the computer processor for both encoding and playback (encoding is usually done with special hardware). MPEG was created for high-end video delivery, so its use for low data-rate Web video has been limited.

MULTIMEDIA RECIPES

AUDIO

1 Record the audio in the best possible setting with the best equipment.
2 Digitize the audio at CD quality – that is, 44.1 kHz, 16-bit stereo.
3 Use sound editing software, such as Macromedia's SoundEdit 16, to edit and mix the audio.
4 Use the equalizing function to boost *slightly* the midrange frequencies.
5 After all editing is complete, normalize the file.
6 Use either the sound editing software or a media tool such as Terran Interactive's Media Cleaner Pro to downsample and compress your audio, and save the resulting file as a fast-start QuickTime file.

SLIDE SHOW

1 Perform steps 1–5 of the audio processing procedure.
2 Use video editing software, such as Adobe Premiere, to synchronize still images with the audio track.
3 Use the Media Cleaner Export module to transfer the edited movie from Premiere to Media Cleaner Pro.
4 Use Media Cleaner Pro to:
   a Compress the audio;
   b Scale the movie to 320 × 240 pixels or smaller;
   c Set the frame rate to 1 frame per second;
   d Set the codec to JPEG;
   e Apply the noise reduction filter;
   f Limit the data rate to 40 KBps;
   g Save the file as a fast-start QuickTime file.

VIDEO

1 Digitize the video at the highest settings achievable with your hardware (full resolution is 640 × 480 pixels, 30 fps, with CD-quality audio).
2 Extract the audio track and perform steps 4–5 of the audio procedure.
3 Use Premiere to synchronize the processed audio with the video track and to perform video editing.
4 Use the Media Cleaner Export module to transfer the edited movie from Premiere to Media Cleaner Pro.
5 Use Media Cleaner Pro to:
   a Compress the audio;
   b Scale the movie to 320 × 240 pixels or smaller;
   c Crop any noise or border from the edges of the movie;
   d Set the movie frame rate (from 6 to 15 fps);
   e Set the codec to Cinepak or Sorenson Video;
   f Apply the noise reduction filter;
   g Limit the data rate to 5 to 40 KBps;
   h Make the file a fast-start QuickTime file.

References

1 PROCESS

Frenza, J., and M. Szabo. 1996. *Web and new media pricing guide*. Indianapolis, Ind.: Hayden Books.

Rosenfeld, L., and P. Morville. 1998. *Information architecture for the World
Wide Web*. Sebastopol, Calif.: O'Reilly.

Sano, D. 1996. *Designing large-scale Web sites: A visual design methodology*.
New York: Wiley.

Siegel, D. 1997. *Secrets of successful Web sites: Project management on the
World Wide Web*. 2d ed. Indianapolis, Ind.: Hayden Books.

2 INTERFACE DESIGN

Interface design and the Web

Rosenfeld, L., and P. Morville. 1998. *Information architecture for the World
Wide Web*. Sebastopol, Calif.: O'Reilly.

Sano, D. 1996. *Designing large-scale Web sites: A visual design methodology*.
New York: Wiley.

Veen, J. 1997. *Hot Wired style: Principles for building smart Web sites*. San
Francisco: Wired Books.

Human-computer interaction

Apple Computer, Inc. 1992. *Macintosh human interface guidelines*. Reading,
Mass.: Addison-Wesley.

Cooper, A. 1995. *About face: The essentials of user interface design*. Foster
City, Calif.: IDG Books.

Mullet, K., and D. Sano. 1995. *Designing visual interfaces: Communication-
oriented techniques*. Mountain View, Calif.: SunSoft Press.

Norman, D. 1988. *The psychology of everyday things*. New York: Basic
Books. [Also sold as *The design of everyday things*.]

Preece, J., Y. Rogers, H. Sharp, and B. Benyon. 1994. *Human-computer interaction*. Reading, Mass.: Addison-Wesley.

Shneiderman, B. 1997. *Designing the user interface: Strategies for effective
human-computer interaction*. 3d ed. Reading, Mass.: Addison-Wesley.

Tufte, E. 1983. *The visual display of quantitative information*. Cheshire,
Conn.: Graphics Press.

Tufte, E. 1990. *Envisioning information*. Cheshire, Conn.: Graphics Press.

Tufte, E. 1997. *Visual explanations: Images and quantities, evidence and narrative*. Cheshire, Conn.: Graphics Press.

3 SITE DESIGN

Rosenfeld, L., and P. Morville. 1998. *Information architecture for the World Wide Web*. Sebastopol, Calif.: O'Reilly.

Sano, D. 1996. *Designing large-scale Web sites: A visual design methodology*. New York: Wiley.

Veen, J. 1997. *Hot Wired style: Principles for building smart Web sites*. San Francisco: Wired Books.

4 PAGE DESIGN

Sano, D. 1996. *Designing large-scale Web sites: A visual design methodology*. New York: Wiley.

Siegel, D. 1997. *Creating killer Web sites*. 2d ed. Indianapolis, Ind.: Hayden Books.

Veen, J. 1997. *Hot Wired style: Principles for building smart Web sites*. San Francisco: Wired Books.

5 TYPOGRAPHY

Bringhurst, R. 1996. *The elements of typographic style*. 2d ed. Vancouver, B.C.: Hartley and Marks.

Burke, C. 1990. *Type from the desktop: Designing with type and your computer*. Research Triangle Park, N.C.: Ventana Press.

Carter, R., B. Day, and A. Miller. 1997. *Typographic design: Form and communication*. 2d ed. New York: Van Nostrand Reinhold.

Lie, H., and B. Bos. 1997. *Cascading Style Sheets: Designing for the Web*. Reading, Mass.: Addison-Wesley.

Raggett, D., J. Lam, I. Alexander, and M. Kmiec. 1998. *Raggett on HTML 4*. 2d ed. Reading, Mass.: Addison-Wesley.

Siegel, D. 1997. *Creating killer Web sites*. 2d ed. Indianapolis, Ind.: Hayden Books.

Spiekermann, E., and E. Ginger. 1993. *Stop stealing sheep and find out how type works*. Mountain View, Calif.: Adobe.

Williams, R. 1990. *The Mac is not a typewriter: A style manual for creating professional-level type on your Macintosh*. Berkeley, Calif.: Peachpit Press.

6 EDITORIAL STYLE

Mullen, R. 1998. *The HTML 4 programmer's reference: All platforms*. Research Triangle Park, N.C.: Ventana Press.

Nielsen, J. 1995. *Alertbox: Jakob Nielsen's column on Web usability*. Internet. Available: http://www.useit.com/alertbox/. 1 October 1997.

Raggett, D., J. Lam, I. Alexander, and M. Kmiec. 1998. *Raggett on HTML 4*. 2d ed. Reading, Mass.: Addison-Wesley.

Strunk, W., and E. White. 1979. *The elements of style*. 3d ed. New York: Macmillan.

Xerox Corporation. 1988. *Xerox publishing standards: A manual of style and design*. New York: Watson-Guptill.

Zinsser, W. 1990. *On writing well: an informal guide to writing nonfiction*. 4th ed. New York: HarperCollins.

7 WEB GRAPHICS

Siegel, D. 1997. *Creating killer Web sites*. 2d ed. Indianapolis, Ind.: Hayden Books.

Webster, T., P. Atzberger, and A. Zolli. 1997. *Web designer's guide to graphics: PNG, GIF, and JPEG*. Indianapolis, Ind.: Hayden Books.

Weinman, L. 1997. *Designing Web graphics: How to prepare images and media for the Web*. 2d ed. Indianapolis, Ind.: New Riders.

8 MULTIMEDIA

Essex, J. 1996. *Multimedia sound and music studio*. New York: Random House.

Held, J. 1988. Making waves with streaming audio. *MacWorld* (February).

Johnson, N. 1997. Getting video on the Web. *DV* (August).

Terran Interactive. 1997. *Media Cleaner Pro User Manual*. San Jose, Calif.: Terran Interactive. [See also http://www.terran-int.com/info/index.html]

Index

Illustration Credits

The following illustrations are reprinted with express permission:

2 INTERFACE DESIGN

www.med.yale.edu   Copyright © 1998 Yale–New Haven Medical Center. Used with express permission.

www.adobe.com   Adobe and the Adobe logo are trademarks of Adobe Systems Incorporated. Copyright © 1998 Adobe Systems Incorporated. Used with express permission.

www.pbs.org/wgbh/nova   Copyright © 1998 WGBH Educational Foundation & PBS.

3 SITE DESIGN

www.ynhh.org   Copyright © 1998 Yale–New Haven Hospital. Used with express permission.

www.hhmi.org   Copyright © 1998 Howard Hughes Medical Institute. Used with express permission.

www.dartmouth.edu/~italo1   Copyright © 1997–1998 Dartmouth College.

info.med.yale.edu/library   Copyright © 1998 Yale University Cushing/Whitney Medical Library. Used with express permission.

www.med.yale.edu   Copyright © 1998 Yale–New Haven Medical Center. Used with express permission.

www.nytimes.com   Copyright © 1998 The New York Times Company. Reprinted by permission.

www.dartmouth.edu   Copyright © 1997–1998 Dartmouth College.

renee.esordi.com   Copyright © 1998 Renee L. Esordi Photography.

www.kodak.com   Courtesy © Eastman Kodak Company, 1994–1998. Photograph copyright © 1998 Phil Borges.

www.w3.org   Copyright © 1997–1998 World Wide Web Consortium (Massachusetts Institute of Technology Laboratory for Computer Science, Institut National de Recherche en Informatique et en Automatique, Keio University). All rights reserved. http://www.w3.org/Consortium/Legal/

thomas.loc.gov   The Library of Congress THOMAS Web site is in the public domain. It contains information about federal legislation.

www.sun.com/service   Copyright © 1994–1998 Sun Microsystems, Inc. All rights reserved. Used by permission. Sun, Sun Microsystems, the Sun logo, Java, and all Sun-based and Java-based trademarks and logos are trademarks or registered trademarks of Sun Microsystems, Inc., in the U.S. and other countries.

4 PAGE DESIGN

www.dartmouth.edu/~cc   Copyright © 1997–1998 Dartmouth College.

www.metadesign.com   Copyright © 1998 MetaDesign.

info.med.yale.edu   Copyright © 1998 Yale–New Haven Medical Center. Used with express permission.

www.ynhh.org   Copyright © 1998 Yale–New Haven Hospital. Used with express permission.

www.iso.ch   Reproduced courtesy of ISO Online.

www.dartmouth.edu/~sources   Copyright © 1998 Dartmouth College.

www.dartmouth.edu/~chemlab   Copyright © 1997–1998 Dartmouth College.

www.dartmouth.edu/~fnchron Copyright © 1998 Malcolm Brown.
www.dartmouth.edu/~milton Copyright © 1997–1998 Dartmouth College.
projects.dartmouth.edu/the_room Copyright © 1997–1998 Dartmouth College.

5 TYPOGRAPHY
www.dartmouth.edu/~cc/didactic Copyright © 1997–1998 Dartmouth College.
www.dartmouth.edu/~hist53 Copyright © 1997–1998 Dartmouth College.
www.dartmouth.edu/~socy15 Copyright © 1998 Dartmouth College.
www.ynhh.org Copyright © 1998 Yale–New Haven Hospital. Used with express
permission.

6 EDITORIAL STYLE
www.dartmouth.edu/~chemlab Copyright © 1997–1998 Dartmouth College.

7 WEB GRAPHICS
info.med.yale.edu Copyright © 1998 Yale–New Haven Medical Center. Used
with express permission.
www.hotwired.com/synapse Copyright © 1994–1998 Wired Digital, Inc. All
rights reserved.
www.sun.com Copyright © 1994–1998 Sun Microsystems, Inc. All rights reserved. Used by permission. Sun, Sun Microsystems, the Sun logo, Java, and all
Sun-based and Java-based trademarks and logos are trademarks or registered
trademarks of Sun Microsystems, Inc., in the U.S. and other countries.

8 MULTIMEDIA
www.jonesandjones.com Copyright © 1997 Jones & Jones Architects and
Landscape Architects. Designed by John Van Dyke.
www.dartmouth.edu/~germ3/rilke Copyright © 1997–1998 Dartmouth College.
Cold Harvest: The Natural Ice Business in Rural Vermont Copyright © 1995
R. Michael Murray.

Designed and typeset by Sarah Horton
Illustrations by Patrick J. Lynch and Sarah Horton

The text face is Goudy, designed in 1915 by
Frederic W. Goudy for the American Type Founders

Captions, code examples, and labels are set in
Syntax, designed by Hans Eduard Meyer in 1968
for the Stempel foundry

Printed by Victor Graphics, Baltimore

Web Style Guide
Basic Design Principles for Creating Web Sites
Patrick J. Lynch and Sarah Horton

THIS ESSENTIAL GUIDE for Web site designers offers clear, concise advice on creating well-designed and effective Web sites and pages. Focusing on the interface and graphic design principles that underlie the best Web site design, the book provides anyone involved with Web site design – in corporations, government, nonprofit organizations, and academic institutions – with expert guidance on issues ranging from planning and organizing goals to design strategies for a site to the elements of individual page design.

Shifting away from the emphasis of many authors on HyperText Markup Language (HTML) and glitzy, gimmicky graphics, Patrick J. Lynch and Sarah Horton discuss classic principles of design, how these principles apply to Web design, and the issues and constraints of designing complex, multilayered sites. They address the practical concerns of bending and adapting HTML to the purposes of graphic page design.

This book grew out of the widely used and highly praised Web site on site design created by the Center for Advanced Instructional Media at Yale University (info.med.yale.edu/caim/manual). At this site, readers will continue to find updated color illustrations and examples to complement and demonstrate points made in the book as well as useful and current online references.

"A style guide for the interface with real long-run value, showing us deep principles of design rather than simply fashion and technology."
– Edward R. Tufte, Yale University

"At last, a book on the design of Web sites with the viewer in mind. . . . [It] intelligently and succinctly discusses all those topics so badly neglected by most Web sites."
– Donald A. Norman, author of *The Design of Everyday Things* and *The Invisible Computer*

"One of the few resources that discusses organizing information on the Web in ways that serve users. This guide addresses a critical need in a practical way."
– Craig Locatis, National Library of Medicine, National Institutes of Health

Patrick J. Lynch is design director of the Center for Advanced Instructional Media at Yale University School of Medicine. Sarah Horton is multimedia specialist in Curricular Computing at Dartmouth College.